# The Thinking Spirit

*Also by*
*John O'Meara*


THE MODERN DEBACLE


SHAKESPEARE'S MUSE

# The Thinking Spirit

## RUDOLF STEINER and Romantic Theory

*A Collection of Texts with Notes*

*by*

*John O'Meara*

iUniverse, Inc.
New York  Lincoln  Shanghai

# The Thinking Spirit
## Rudolf Steiner and Romantic Theory

Copyright © 2007 by John O'Meara

iUniverse books may be ordered through booksellers or by contacting:

iUniverse
2021 Pine Lake Road, Suite 100
Lincoln, NE 68512
www.iuniverse.com
1-800-Authors (1-800-288-4677)

Because of the dynamic nature of the Internet, any Web addresses or links contained in this book may have changed since publication and may no longer be valid.

The views expressed in this work are solely those of the author and do not necessarily reflect the views of the publisher, and the publisher hereby disclaims any responsibility for them.

ISBN: 978-0-595-45714-4 (pbk)
ISBN: 978-0-595-90015-2 (ebk)

Printed in the United States of America

# *Contents*

For
BODO Von PLATO
for appearing to me once
in a dream to admonish me:
"What else is there for us to do?"

During the last decades of the nineteenth-century the Austrian-born RUDOLF STEINER (1861-1925) became a respected and well-published scientific, literary, and philosophical scholar, particularly known for his work on Goethe's scientific writings. After the turn of the century he began to develop his earlier philosophical principles into an approach to methodical research of psychological and spiritual phenomena.

His multi-faceted genius has led to innovative and holistic approaches in medicine, science, education (the Waldorf schools), special education, philosophy, religion, economics, agriculture (the Bio-dynamic method), architecture, drama, the art of eurythmy, and other fields. In 1924 he founded the General Anthroposophical Society, which today has branches throughout the world.

[from the Anthroposophical Press]

The author wishes to thank the various anthroposophical presses, and especially Mercury Press, for permission to draw on their translations of Rudolf Steiner's texts.

Acknowledgments also to Luigi Luzio, for his intense interest and support in the initial stages of this work, and for saving the one copy of it that existed at one time.

# *Preface*

The present collection of texts aims to relate the work of Rudolf Steiner to what is perhaps the best known product of romantic theory in English—S.T. Coleridge's theory of the Imagination, as set forth in the twelfth and thirteenth chapters of the *Biographia Literaria*. My purpose is to make good my claim, in an earlier book, for a fulfilment and continuation of Romantic tradition in the theory of Steiner.[1] The Romantic epoch, as we have known it, has by now come to an end; it came to an end because the creative thought that served that epoch could not fully satisfy the requirements of thinking or the further necessity of theory that properly characterize our own age. But Romantic tradition continues, with the full theory and culture of thinking elaborated by Steiner, who himself should satisfy our sense of what is required to support a recovery of the Imagination in our own time.

Coleridge's connection to Steiner is made clear at once when one sets the former's text from the *Biographia* in the midst of a careful selection of writings taken from the first fifteen years of Steiner's theoretical production (from 1882-1897). Even among those directly engaged in carrying forward the work begun in association with Rudolf Steiner, it is still not sufficiently recognized that his work emerges as a direct and entirely natural evolution of Western intellectual thinking up to his time, or that he himself was bent on establishing that this was so, devoting the greater part of twenty years, and more, to this arduous task. At the heart of this production is a long series of introductions to Goethe's natural-scientific work brought together in *Goethean Science*, which contains some of the most important material Steiner produced in this period. At one end of this period is Steiner's first comprehensive declaration of theory—his *Science of Knowing* (1886)—put out within four years of undertaking his work as an editor of Goethe. At the other end of this period is *Goethe's World View* (1897), serving as recapitulation of this work and containing the crucial 'critique of Goethe'. In the

---

1.    See *Othello's Sacrifice: Essays on Shakespeare and Romantic Tradition* (Toronto: Guernica, 1996).

meantime, Steiner had also written *The Philosophy of Freedom* (1894), thus already making good on this critique.

In what follows, I bring Coleridge forward in the context of a selection principally from these four texts. The selection is designed to show the astonishing integrity, depth and breadth of Steiner's theoretical position in his work of this period. From the juxtaposition, one appreciates, at the same time, how Coleridge, in the twelfth and thirteenth chapters of the *Biographia*, directly anticipates the whole of Steiner's later work of this time. What follows stops short at those areas of the early work by Steiner that may still be said to be for the most part directly engaged in the production of theory, though Steiner's later work is, of course, replete with reminders of theory. Beyond this, we should need to follow Steiner further in the continuous transvaluation of our thinking which his work represents from stage to stage. The story of that transvaluation begins, as we shall see, with Steiner's study of Goethe. It is the story to which Coleridge himself would have wished to belong.

# Works Cited

(BL) *Biographia Literaria*, ed., James Engell and W. Jackson Bate (Princeton: Princeton University Press, 1983)

(CMF) *Christianity as Mystical Fact* (Hudson, New York: Anthroposophic Press, 1972)

(GS) *Goethean Science*, tr., William Lindeman (Spring Valley, New York: Mercury Press, 1988)

(GWV) *Goethe's World View*, tr., William Lindeman (Spring Valley, New York: Mercury Press, 1992)

(KHW) *Knowledge of the Higher Worlds*, tr., D.S. Osmond and C. Davy (London: Rudolf Steiner Press, 1969)

(OS) *Occult Science*, tr., Maud and Henry B. Monges and Lisa D. Monges (Spring Valley, New York: Anthroposophic Press, 1985)

(PF) *The Philosophy of Freedom*, tr. Michael Wilson (London: Rudolf Steiner Press, 1964)

(SK) *The Science of Knowing*, tr., William Lindeman (Spring Valley, New York: Mercury Press, 1988)

(TH) *Theosophy*, tr., Henry B. Monges (Hudson, New York: Anthroposophic Press, 1988)

# A Note on Editorial Conventions

In the text that follows in many instances I have culled Steiner's statements from mid-sentence. It did not seem right, in those instances, to capitalize the first word, *or* to burden the text with a widespread use of elliptical notation to advertise that kind of case, and so the absence of punctuation where these statements begin and end. Where a capital *is* used to mark the beginning of a statement, the reader should understand that Steiner's statement begins as a sentence in his own text. However, it may also be that the statement ends in mid-sentence, which explains why the reader, in this case also, will find no punctuation where the statement ends.

It has also seemed to me right to break up Steiner's statements because each of these requires more than usual pondering, and also to facilitate observation of the continuity across the statements, as well as the main lines of argument.

Different sections of argument are more obviously marked by formal breaks in the text.

Yet another set of conventions governs the presentation of *Knowledge of the Higher Worlds*, duly noted in footnote 5 on page 82.

*Today there is only one way of preserving the personality, and that is ... to compre-hend the spiritual world out of the present intellectual standards ...*
—Rudolf Steiner

*The resolve to philosophize is a summons to the true ego that it shall awaken to self-awareness and be a spirit.*
—Novalis

*Meantime within man is the soul of the whole ...*
—Emerson

# PART I
# The Living Principle of Knowledge

*If the man is true to his better instincts or sentiments, and refuses the dominion of facts, as one that comes of a higher race, remains fast by the soul and sees the principle, then the facts fall aptly and supple into their places; they know their master, and the meanest of them glorifies him.*

*For the soul will not have us read any other cipher than that of cause and effect.*

—Emerson, "History"[1]

---

1.  All quotations from Emerson are taken from *Self-Reliance and Other Essays* (New York: Dover Publications, 1993).

# 1

# *Goethe's World View and Its Extension as Science*

From Steiner's *Goethean Science*

we can very often find already in the indications we have about [Goethe's] thinking from 1769-1775 the germs of his later works

He was developing for himself the idea of a being in which each part enlivens the other, in which one principle imbues all the particulars.[1] (GS,6)

This being is conceived of as subject to continuous changes in time, but in all the stages of these changes only one being is always manifesting itself, a being that asserts itself as what endures, as what is constant within the change.[2]

---

1.    Here Steiner quotes from *Faust*, (Part I, Night):
      *Into the whole how all things blend*
      *Each in the other working, living!*

      Also from *Satyros* (Act IV):
      *How from no-thing the primal thing arose,*
      *How power of light through the night did ring,*
      *Imbuing the depths of the beings all;*
      *Thus welled up desiring's surge.*
      *And the elements disclosed themselves,*
      *With hunger into one another poured,*
      *All-imbuing, all-imbued.*

2.    From *Satyros*:
      *And rolling up and down did go*
      *The all and one eternal thing,*
      *Ever changing, ever constant.*

the entire universe is pictured as such a living being. (GS,7)

his view of the entire world as one great organism.... confronts us once more in *Faust* at that place where the earth spirit is represented as that life principle which permeates the universal organism[3] (GS,8)

in his essay, *Nature*, written about 1780.... [t]he idea confronts us of a being that is caught up in constant change and yet remains thereby ever the same: "All is new and ever the old."

each of ... [Nature's] works has its own being, each of her manifestations has the most isolated concept, and yet all constitute one.[4]

---

Goethe had already developed for himself a definite concept of an organism before he came to Weimar.

[But he] had not yet applied this concept to any particular genus of natural objects (GS,9)

With respect to scientific study, the young Goethe [to 1776] seems altogether to be like Faust, deprived of the freshness of firsthand beholding of nature, who expresses his longing for this [in Part I, Night] (GS,10)

---

3.    From Part I, Night:
          *In the tides of life, in actions' storm,*
          *Up and down I wave,*
          *To and fro weave free,*
          *Birth and the grave,*
          *An infinite sea,*
          *A varied weaving,*
          *A radiant living.*
4.    With this view Goethe was recovering the venerable and longstanding idea of the many and the one. In "Parabasis" (c.1820), Goethe would describe it again as "the One Eternal-Multiply self-manifest". All subsequent quotations from Goethe, unless by Steiner, are from the *Selected Poems*, ed., Christopher Middleton (London: John Calder, 1983).

Now, the most important thing of all was to develop this lasting, this constant element, this archetypal form with which nature, as it were, plays—to develop it in detail into a plastic configuration.[5] (GS,15)

the constant element must be sought in something else that underlies [the] changeable outer aspects…. in the lawfulness manifesting in the organism, the animalness of the animal, the life that gives form to itself out of itself, that has the power and ability—through the possibilities lying within it—to develop itself in manifold outer shapes (species, genera)[6] (GS,16)

---

the main thing to keep in mind about the organism is the fact … that the whole works in every organ. (GS,5)

The fact that one particular state is brought forth first and another one last is determined in the nature of the whole; and the sequence of the intermediary states is also determined by the idea of the whole; what comes before is dependent on what comes after, and vice-versa; in short, within the living organism, there is development from one thing out of the other.[7] (GS,19)

---

In the plant, this determination of each individual member by the whole arises insofar as every organ is built according to the same basic form.

"It became clear to me, namely, that within that organ (of the plant) that we usually address as leaf, there lies hidden the true Proteus that can conceal and manifest itself in every shape.[8] Anyway you look at it, the plant is always only leaf, so inseparably joined with the future germ that one cannot think the one without the other." [Goethe to Herder, May, 1787]

The plant is therefore a being that successively develops certain organs that are all—both in their interrelationships and in the relationship of each to the whole—built according to one and the same idea. (GS,20)

---

5.  As Nature does.
6.  Thus 'lawful development' connects the many to the one.
7.  'Lawful development' from first to last.
8.  Note the emphasis here on that "within" the leaf, i.e., the 'idea' in the leaf.

from Steiner's *Goethe's World View*

"everything is leaf[9], and through this simplicity the greatest manifoldness becomes possible." (GWV,90)

[Goethe] feels impelled to know the developmental laws of animal form in the same way

He is convinced that the unity of the animal organism also rests on one basic organ which can assume various forms in outer phenomena. (GWV,100)

Goethe did not succeed in drawing together the lawfulness of the entire animal form into one single mental picture as he was able to do for the plant form.[10]

He found the developmental law of one part of this form only, the spinal cord and brain, along with the bones which enclose these organs.

He sees in the brain a higher development of the spinal cord

Every ganglion, every nerve center, represents for him a brain which has remained behind on a lower level

And he interprets the skull bones which enclose the brain as transformations of the vertebrae which surround the spinal cord. (GWV,101)

From *Goethean Science*

The whole head appears in this way to be prefigured in the bodily organs that stand at a lower level.

This was a discovery of the most far-reaching significance. It showed that all the parts of an organic whole are identical with respect to idea, that 'inwardly unformed' organic masses open themselves up outwardly in different ways and

---

9.   In idea; note also the stress on "this" in what follows.
10.  Because there are in fact three systems in the animal: head, heart and digestive systems, all of which combine in yet another way in man. See Steiner, *Man as Symphony of the Creative Word* (1924).

that it is one and the same thing that—at a lower level as spinal cord nerve and on a higher level as sense nerve—opens itself up into the sense organ (GS,44)

This discovery revealed every living thing in its power to form and give shape to itself from within outward; only then was it grasped as something truly living. (GS,45)

---

from *Goethe's World View*

Goethe did not succeed in progressing from this felicitous starting-point to the laws of development of the whole animal form.

nothing analogous to the archetypal plant emerged.

Goethe could not develop a unified mental picture of how an archetypal image, by lawful transformation of one basic part, develops itself as the archetypal form, with many parts, of the animal organism.[11] (GWV,103)

still Goethe did succeed in finding individual laws to which nature holds in the development of animal forms

If nature develops and forms one part with particular completeness, this can happen only at the expense of another part.

In the individual animal form one part is developed, another part is only suggested; one is particularly well-developed, another is perhaps totally imperceptible to sense-observation.[12]

In this last case, Goethe is convinced that that part of the general prototype which is not visible in each animal is nevertheless present as idea. (GWV,104)

In the archetypal organism all the parts are developed and maintain a balance with each other; the diversity of the individual organisms arises through the fact

---

11. "archetypal image"—or 'idea'; "by lawful transformation of one basic part", the 'idea' becomes the object of 'science'.
12. A process (processes) demonstrated with astonishing completeness of vision by Steiner himself in *Man as Symphony*.

that the formative power expends itself on one part and therfore does not develop the outer manifestation of another part at all or only suggests it.

Today one calls this law of the animal organism the law of correlation or compensation of organs. (GWV,105)

---

From *Goethean Science*

Now we must also still bear in mind that while these views were developing ever more definitely in Goethe, he stood in lively communication with Herder, who in 1783 began to write his *Ideas on a Philosophy of the History of Mankind.* (GS,28)

many an idea must be traced back to Goethe

in the first part of his book, Herder holds the following view

A principle form must be presupposed that runs through all beings and realizes itself in different ways.

An ideal typical form, which as such is not itself sense-perceptibly real, realizes itself in an endless number of spatially separated entities with differing characteristics all the way up to man.

At the lower levels of organization, this ideal form always realizes itself in a particular direction; the ideal form develops in a particular way according to this direction.

When this typical form ascends as far as man, it brings together all the developmental principles—which it had always developed only in a one-sided way in the lower organisms and had distributed among different entities—in order to form *one* shape.

From this ... follows the possibility of such high perfection in the human being.

In man's case, nature bestowed upon one being what, in the case of the animals, it had dispersed among many classes and orders.

---

This thought worked with unusual fruitfulness upon the German philosophy that followed.

let us mention here the description that Oken later gave of the same idea.... [in] his *Textbook of Natural Philosophy* (GS,29)

"The animal realm is only *one* animal.... the animal realm is merely the dismembered highest animal—man.

There is only one human kind, only one human race, only one human species, just because man is the whole animal realm."

---

with every species of animal, one organ system comes one-sidedly to the fore; the whole animal merges into it; everything else about the animal recedes into the background.

Now in human development, all the organs and organ systems develop in such a way that one allows the other enough space to develop freely

each one retires within those boundaries that seem necessarily to allow all the others to come into their own in the same way.

These thoughts ... formed the content of the conversations of Goethe with Herder, and Herder gives expression to them in the following way:

"man is a central creation among the animals ... he is the elaborated form in which the traits of all the species gather around him in their finest essence."[13] (GS,30)

---

13. *Man as Symphony* (delivered over thirty years after this commentary by Steiner) should be seen as fulfilling this line of thought.

It is true that Goethe made a number of great single discoveries, such as the inter-maxillary bone, the vertebral theory of the skull in osteology, the common identity of all plant organs with the leaf in botany.

But we have to regard as the life and soul of all these individual cases the magnificent view of nature by which they are carried

we have to fix our attention above all on a magnificent discovery that overshadows everything else: that of the being of the organism itself.[14]

Goethe has set forth the principle by which an organism is what it presents itself to be

he sets forth, in fact, everything we can ask about the manifestations of life from a point of view concerned with principles. (GS,1)

To what extent there lived in Goethe the thought of presenting his views on nature in a larger work becomes particularly clear to us when we see that, with every new discovery he achieves, he cannot keep from expressly raising the possibility to his friends of extending his thoughts out over the whole of nature. (GS,36)

From *Goethe's World View*

One can guess, from Goethe's sketchy *Outline of a Morphology* which still exists, that he planned to present in their successive levels the particular shapes which his archetypal plant and archetypal animal assume in the main forms of living beings.

He wanted first of all to describe the being of the organic as it came to him in his reflections about animals and plants.

Then, "starting at one point", to show how the archetypal organic being develops itself on the one hand into the manifold plant world, on the other into the multiplicity of the animal forms

---

14.  I.e., one life in many forms.

how the particular forms of the worms, insects, higher animals, and the human form can be drawn forth from the common archetypal picture.[15] (GWV,112)

From Steiner's *Goethean Science*

[quoting Goethe]

"Since I had, after all, ceaselessly pressed on, at first unconsciously and out of an inner urge, toward that primal archetypal element, since I had even succeeded in building up a presentation of this which was in accordance with nature, nothing more could keep me then from courageously undertaking the adventure of reason, as the old man of Konigsberg [i.e., Kant] himself calls it." (GS,55)

from *Goethean Science*

It is a great pity that such a work from Goethe's hand did not come about. To judge by everything we have, it would have been a creation far surpassing everything of this sort that has been done in recent times.

It would have become a canon from which every endeavor in the field of natural science would have to take its start and against which one could test the spiritual content of such an endeavor.

We would have had to do here with the work of a spirit in whom no one individual branch of the human endeavor pushes itself forward at the expense of all the others, but rather in whom the totality of human existence always hovers in the background when he is dealing with one particular area. (GS,36)

This strictest objectivity would make Goethe's work the most perfect work of natural science ... for the philosopher, it would be an archetypal model of how to find the laws of objective contemplation of the world.[16]

---

15. *Man as Symphony* fulfils this great plan.
16. As it was for Hegel.

Goethe himself gives the reason why this work did not come about: "The task was so great that it could not be accomplished in a scattered life".[17] (GS,37)

---

in the main Goethe and Herder were in agreement all that time [1783 and after] with respect to their views about the place of the human being in nature.

But this basic view requires now that every organ, every part of an animal, must also be able to be found again in man, only pushed back within the limits determined by the harmony of the whole.

This is how the matter stood with Goethe, when all at once he became aware of a view that totally contradicted this great thought.

The difference between animals and man was supposed to consist in the fact that the former have a little bone, the intermaxillary bone between the two symmetrical halves of the upper jaw, which holds the upper incisors and supposedly is lacking in man. (GS,31)

By virtue of his whole spiritual orientation, Goethe could not think otherwise than that an intermaxillary bone must also be present in man.

It was only a matter of proving this empirically, of finding what form this bone takes in man and to what extent it adapts itself to the whole of his organism.

Now this individual discovery, compared to the great thought by which it is sustained, should not be overvalued: for Goethe also, its value lay only in the fact that it cleared away a preconception that seemed to hinder his ideas from being consistently pursued right into the farthest details of an organism. (GS,33)

---

17.   Steiner's forward-looking account of Goethe's plan Steiner himself would fulfil in his work as a whole. We may compare with this the standard academic judgment of this plan as 'lost cause' as given, e.g., by H.B. Nisbet in *Goethe and the Scientific Tradition* (Institute of Germanic Studies, University of London, 1972). One may see in this nice, academic reduction of romantic potential both a symptom and a cause of the decline of the Romantic epoch: "the individual in search of fuller development, of the ability to look at things in a more comprehensive way" (p.74), who yet is without a sense of the 'whole man' whose fall he has *accepted*. (p.73)

Goethe also never regarded it as an individual discovery, but always only in connection with his larger view of nature.

Thus he writes to Knebel in November 1784, when he sends him the treatise on his discovery: "I have refrained from showing yet the result, to which Herder already points in his ideas, which is, namely, that one cannot find the difference between man and animal in the details." (GS,34)

Herder writes about this to Knebel: "Goethe has presented me with his treatise on the bone; it is very simple and beautiful; the human being travels the true path of nature and fortune comes to meet him." (GS,40)

# 2

## *Knowing in Goethe's Sense*

from *Goethean Science*

[Goethe] everywhere seeks not only what is given to the senses in the outer world, but also the tendency through which it has come into being.... just as the mathematician always keeps his eye, not upon this or that particular triangle, but always upon that lawfulness which underlies every possible triangle.

The point is not *what* nature has created but rather the principle by which nature has created it. (GS,100)

Then this principle is to be developed in the way that accords with its own nature, and not in the way this has occurred in each particular entity of nature in accordance with thousands of chance factors. (GS,101)

---

Kant believed that philosophy before him had taken wrong paths

one reflected upon the nature of the object to be known before one had examined the activity of knowing itself, with regard to what it could do.

He therefore took this latter examination as his basic philosophical problem and inaugurated thereby a new direction in thought.

But what if the concept of knowledge that Kant and his followers have, and about which they ask if it is possible or not, proved to be totally untenable; what if this concept could not stand up to a penetrating critique? (GS,105)

one will be able to make nothing out of the possibility of knowledge until one has answered the question as to the *what* of knowing itself.

———————————————

The forming of a particular judgment, the establishing of a fact or series of facts—which according to Kant one could already call knowledge—is not yet by any means knowing in Goethe's sense.

*distancing* of oneself from the sense world in all its directness is indicative of Goethe's view of real knowing.

The directly given is experience. In our knowing, however, we create a picture of the directly given that contains considerably more than what the senses ... can provide. (GS,106)

The question now confronts us: How does what is directly experienced relate to the picture of experience that arises in the process of knowing? (GS,107)

Let us [turn] to the example of the thrown stone. We connect the sight perceptions that originate from the individual locations in which the stone finds itself. This connection gives us a curved line (the trajectory), and we obtain the laws of trajectory; when furthermore we take into account the material composition of the glass, and then understand the flying stone as *cause*, the shattering of the glass as *effect*, and so on, we then have permeated the given with concepts in such a way that it becomes comprehensible to us.

This entire operation, which draws together the manifoldness of perception into a conceptual *unity*, occurs within our consciousness. The ideal interrelationship of the perceptual pictures is not given by the senses, but rather is grasped absolutely on its own by our spirit. (GS,109)

For a being endowed only with the ability to perceive with the senses, the whole operation would simply not be there. For such a being the outer world would simply remain that disconnected chaos of perceptions we characterized as what first (directly) confronts us.

[1]Now, even though this conceptual (lawful) relationship, in its substantial make-up, is produced within human consciousness, it by no means follows from this that it is also only subjective in its significance.

It springs, rather, in its *content*, just as much from the objective world as, in its conceptual *form*, it springs from human consciousness.

Precisely because the perceptual picture is something incomplete, something unfinished in itself, we are compelled to add to this picture, in its manifestation as sense experience, its necessary complement. (GS,110)

There the human spirit steps in.

Knowing means: to add the perception of thinking to the half reality of sense experience so that this picture of half reality becomes complete. (GS,111)

---

We will first become clear about this relationship when we investigate why we are unsatisfied by perceptible reality, but are satisfied, on the other hand, by a thought-through reality.

We feel ourselves confronted by a foreign entity that we have not produced, at whose production we were not even, in fact, present. We stand before something that has already come about.[2]

A thought-configuration does not come before me unless I myself participate in its coming about; it comes into the field of my perception only through the fact that I myself lift it up, out of the dark abyss of imperceptibility.

The thought does not arise in me as a finished entity the way a sense perception does, but rather I am conscious of the fact that, when I do hold fast to a concept

---

1.    Here follow two of Steiner's most crucial statements from *Goethean Science*, containing the essence of the view he was to develop at great length.
2.    Here Steiner confronts the basic riddle with which Romantic philosophy was faced; and we note the entirely unique way in which Steiner addresses this riddle.

in its complete form, I myself have brought it into this form.... the completion of a process so integrally merged with me that I have always stood within it.[3]

But this is what I must demand of a thing that enters the horizon of my perception, in order to understand it.... I myself must follow it to that stage at which it has become something finished. (GS,120)

---

This is why the direct form of reality, which we usually call experience, moves us to work it through in knowledge.

When we bring our thinking into movement, we then go back to the determining factors of the given that at first remained hidden to us; we work our way up from the product to the production; we arrive at the stage where sense perception becomes transparent to us in the same way the thought is.

A process of the world appears completely penetrated by us only when the process is our own activity. A thought appears as the completion of a process within which we stand.

---

To investigate the essential being of a thing means to begin at the center of the thought-world and to work from there until a thought-configuration appears before our soul that seems to us to be identical to the thing we are experiencing.

When we speak of the essential being of a thing or of the world altogether, we cannot therefore mean anything else at all than the grasping of reality as thought, as idea.

In the idea we recognize that from which we must derive everything else: the principle of things.

What philosophers call the absolute, the eternal being, the ground of the world, what the religions call God, this we call, on the basis of our epistemological studies: the idea.

---

3.    No one held to this fact more fully or uncompromisingly than did Steiner, as we shall see below.

[4]Everything in the world that does not appear directly as idea will still ultimately be recognized as going forth from the idea.

Nothing may remain away from it; everything must become a part of the great whole that the idea encompasses. (GS,121)

---

I have not arrived at my world view only through the study of Goethe

I took my start from the mechanistic-naturalistic conception of the world, but recognized that, with intensive thinking, one cannot remain there.

Proceeding strictly according to natural-scientific methods, I found in *objective idealism* the only satisfying world view.

My epistemology shows the way by which a kind of thinking that understands itself and is not self-contradictory arrives at this world view.

I then found that this objective idealism, in its basic features, permeates the Goethean world view. (GS,93)

What is *objectively* given by no means coincides with what is *sense-perceptibly* given, as the mechanistic world conception believes.

What is sense-perceptibly given is only half of the given. The other half of the given is ideas, which are also objects of experience—of a higher experience to be sure, whose organ is thinking. (GS,91)

---

Schiller recognized right away the ideal nature of Goethe's archetypal plant and declared that no reality could be consistent with such a plant.

This stimulated Goethe to think about the relationship of what he called 'typus' to empirical reality.... the problem of the relationship between idea and reality, between thinking and experience.

---

4.     There now follow two outstanding deductions, further developed below.

This became ever clearer to him: No one single empirical object corresponds entirely to his typus.

The content of the typus concept cannot therefore stem *from* the sense world as such, even though it is won *in the encounter with* the sense world. (GS,76)

the idea of the archetypal entity could only be of a kind which by virtue of a necessity lying within itself, develops a content out of itself that then in another form—in the form of a perception—manifests within the phenomenal world. (GS,77)

When the typus now enters into manifestation, the truly (no longer intuitive) sense-perceptible form can correspond fully to that ideal or not; the typus can come to its full development or not.

The lower organisms are indeed lower through the fact that their form of manifestation does not fully correspond with the organic typus.

The more that outer manifestation and organic typus coincide in a given entity, the more highly developed it is.

---

It is the task of any systematics to demonstrate this relationship with respect to the form of every organism.

in arriving at the typus it can only be a matter of finding a form that represents the most perfect expression of the typus.

Goethe's archetypal plant is meant to provide such a form. (GS,72)

from *Goethe's World View*

Goethe had developed within him the mental picture of a malleable-ideal form which reveals itself to the spirit when it looks out over the manifoldness of plant shapes and is attentive to what they have in common.

Schiller contemplated this formation, which supposedly lived not in one single plant but rather in all plants, and said, shaking his head, "That is not an experience, that is an idea."

[Goethe] could not respond with anything other than, "I can be very glad, then, when I have ideas without knowing it, and in fact even see them with my eyes."

Goethe sees in the idea of a thing an element that is immediately present within the thing, working and creating in it.

In his view, an individual thing takes on particular forms because the idea must, in a given case, live itself out in a specific way.

Schiller thinks otherwise. For him the world of ideas and the world of experience are two separate realms. (GWV,12)

For Goethe there is only one source of knowledge, the world of experience, in which the world of ideas is included.

For him it is impossible to say, "experience <u>and</u> idea".[5] (GWV,13)

---

5.    A distinction cannot be drawn between "experience and idea" because (for Goethe, as for Steiner) "the idea…is immediately present within the thing". But it is only because a distinction *is* maintained between idea and sense perception (or thing) that further attention can be given to the sense perception without fear—since what is "objectively given" is not what is "sense-perceptibly given". Sense perception (or thing) being a manifestation of the idea, it is as much a part of what is given as the idea itself. The result is a full notion of 'experience' unique in the tradition of Romantic philosophical thinking.

The notion is outlined in Goethe's "Epirrhema":
*You must, when contemplating nature,*
*Attend to this, in each and every feature:*
*There's nought outside and nought within,*
*For she is inside out and outside in.*
*Thus will you grasp, with no delay,*
*The holy secret, clear as day.*

Also, in "True Enough: To a Physicist":
*Nature has neither core*
*Nor outer rind*
*Being all things at once.*

Goethe is convinced that man, in his world of ideas, experiences directly how the creative being of nature does things:

"we would makes ourselves worthy, through beholding an ever-creating nature, of participating spiritually in its productions." (GWV,55)

# 3

## *Overcoming Dualism*

*Men have looked away from themselves and at things so long.*

—Emerson, "Self-Reliance"

From *Goethe's World View*

The separation of idea and perception is justified only when one speaks of how human knowledge comes about.

Plato became conscious of what weight the fact has for man's world view that the world reveals itself to the human being from two sides. Out of his insightful valuation of this fact he recognized that reality cannot be attributed to the sense world, regarded only by itself.

Only when the world of ideas lights up out of his soul life, and man, in looking at the world, can place before his spirit idea and sense observation as a unified knowledge experience does he have true reality before him. (GWV,16)

Platonism is the conviction that the goal of all striving for knowledge must be to acquire the ideas which carry the world and which constitute its foundation.

---

Insofar as Platonism has taken hold in the evolution of Western thought, however, it shows still another side.

Plato did not stop short at emphasizing the knowledge that, in human perception the sense world becomes a mere semblance if the light of the world of ideas is not shone upon it, but rather, through the way he presented this fact, he furthered the belief that the sense world, in and for itself, irrespective of man, is a world of semblance, and that true reality is to be found only in ideas.

Out of this belief there arises the question: how do idea and sense world (nature) come together outside the human being?

for the Goethean world view.... the question: What relationship exists *outside of man* between idea and the sense world?" is an unhealthy one, because for it there is no sense world (nature) without idea outside of man.

Only man can detach the idea from the sense world for himself and thus *picture* nature to be devoid of idea.

for the Goethean world view, the question, "How do idea and sense-perceptible things come together?", which has occupied the evolution of Western thought for centuries, is an entirely superfluous question. (GWV,17)

---

from *Goethean Science*

that view ... that denies to the concept or idea any independent content.... believes ... that the conceptual unity as such is altogether without any content; that this unity arises solely through the fact that certain characteristics of the objects of experience are left aside and that what they have in common, on the other hand, is lifted out and incorporated into our intellect so that we may comfortably bring together the manifoldness of objective reality according to the principle of grasping all of experience with the mind in the fewest possible general unities—i.e., according to the principle of the smallest measure of force. Along with modern natural philosophy, Schopenhauer takes this standpoint. (GS,113)

from *Goethe's World View*

Kant agrees with Hume with respect to his assertion that the ideas into which thinking combines the individual perceptions do not stem from experience, but rather that thinking adds them to experience.

Man possesses necessary truths.

They cannot stem from experience, because it has nothing like them to offer.

In spite of this, man applies them to experience. It lies in his nature to bring the things into the kind of relationship which corresponds to the truths gained by pure thinking. (GWV,27)

these truths relate merely to the way man, of himself, determines his world of experience. They contain the laws of his organization. They have no connection to the things-in-themselves [about which man can experience nothing.]

---

The human being ... does not have to do with the things-in-themselves but only with the impressions which they make upon him and with the relationships into which he himself brings these impressions. (GWV,28)

Kant negated the possibility of our being able to know anything about the reality of the world of ideas from its relationship to sense-perception.

From this presupposition he arrived at the scientific result, which, unknown to him, was demanded by the direction of his religious feeling: that scientific knowledge must come to a halt before the kind of questions which relate to freedom, immortality, and the divine world order.

He wanted to limit knowing in order to preserve a place for faith. (GWV,30)

---

from *Goethean Science*

It will not do to assume higher forms of existence than those belonging to the world of ideas.

Only because the human being is often not able to comprehend that the existence of the idea is something far higher and fuller than that of perceptual reality, does he still seek a further reality.

All the realists make the same mistake (GS,137)

the philosophy of Kant, Schopenhauer, and the neo-Kantians … the last phase of Schelling's philosophy … All these directions of thought are in agreement about seeking the essence of the world in something transsubjective[1], and about having to admit, from their standpoint, that the subjective ideal world … has no significance for reality itself, but purely and simply for human consciousness alone. (GS,112)

This view … assumes the existence of two completely separate worlds. The objective outer world, which bears its essential being, the ground of its existence, within itself, and the subjective-ideal inner world which is supposedly a conceptual copy of the outer world. (GS,111)

The inner world is a matter of no concern to the objective world, is not required by it; the inner world is present only for the knowing human being.

To bring about a [transsubjective] congruence of these two worlds would be the epistemological ideal of this basic view. (GS,112)

------------------

from *The Science of Knowing*

There are two kinds of dogma: the dogma of revelation and that of experience.

The situation with the dogma of experience is quite similar…. Here too the truth is not attained through insight into the inner workings of the things, but rather is imposed by something external to the thing itself.

Whereas the dogma of revelation ruled earlier science, present-day science suffers from the dogma of experience. (SK,72)

from *Goethean Science*

but we also have to reject that false idealism which believes that because we do not get outside of the idea, we also do not get outside of our consciousness, and

------------------

1.    In the case of Kant—faith; Schelling—a personal God; Schopenhauer—the bodily will.

that all the mental pictures given us and the whole world are only subjective illusion, only a dream that our consciousness dreams. (Fichte)

These idealists also do not comprehend that although we do not get outside of the idea, we do nevertheless have *in* the idea something objective that has its basis in itself and not in the subject. (GS,138)

_____

Our standpoint is idealism, because it sees in the idea the ground of the world; it is realism because it addresses the idea as the real; and it is positivism or empiricism because it wants to arrive at the content of the idea not through *a priori* constructions, but rather as something given.

We do not recognize as valid any inferring, from something given and known to us, of an underlying, non-given, determinative element.

We reject any inference in which any part of the inference is not given.

Inferring is only a going from given elements over to other equally given elements. (GS,139)

from *Goethe's World View*

Cf. Goethe:

"Theory, in and for itself, is of no use, but only inasmuch as it makes us believe in the connections of phenomena" (GWV,49)

"because the phenomena are ultimately constrained to connect themselves to each other, or rather to reach over into each other" (GWV,37)

"do not seek anything behind the phenomena; they are themselves the teaching." (GWV,54).

# 4

# *On Thinking as Higher Experience within Experience*

from *Science of Knowing*

A science of knowledge established in the sense of the Goethean world view lays its chief emphasis on the fact that it remains absolutely true to the principle of experience.

No one recognized better than Goethe the total validity of this principle.

All higher views on nature had to appear to him in no form other than as experience.

In his essay "Nature," Goethe says that we are incapable of getting outside nature. If we therefore wish to explain nature to ourselves in his sense, we must find the means of doing so within nature. (SK,37)

---

That we stick to experience is a justified demand of science. But no less so is the demand that we seek out the inner lawfulness of experience. (SK,36)

how could one found a science of knowing upon the principle of experience if in experience itself we did not find at any point the basic element of what is scientific: ideal lawfulness? (SK,37)

This inner being itself must therefore appear at some place in experience as experience.

---

[1]Our epistemology finds, within experience, even the characterizations that thinking makes. (SK,36)

Since we experience a real lawfulness, an ideal definement, only in thinking, the lawfulness of the rest of the world, which we do not experience from this world itself, must also lie already contained in thinking. (SK,40)

What, for the rest of experience, must first be brought from somewhere else—if it is applicable to experience at all—namely, lawful interconnection, is already present in thinking in its very first appearance. (SK,35)

our thinking … on the one hand … manifests as an activity of our consciousness, on the other as a direct manifestation of a lawfulness complete in itself, as self-determined ideal content. (SK,39)

We grasp thought *a* and thought *b* and give them the opportunity to enter into a lawful connection by bringing them into mutual interconnection with each other.

It is not our subjective organization that determines this particular connection between *a* and *b* in precisely one way and no other. (SK,40)

The human spirit effects the joining of thought-masses only in accordance with their content.

In thinking we therefore fulfill the principle of experience in its most basic form.

Here we see which of the two aspects of the thought-world is the essential one: the objective aspect of its content, and not the subjective aspect of the way it arises. (SK,41)

---

This insight into the inner soundness and completeness of thinking appears most clearly in the scientific system of Hegel.

---

1.    The following statements should be referred back to Steiner's commentary on p.15 from "The question now confronts us…"

No one has credited thinking, to the degree he did, with a power so complete that it could found a world view out of itself.

But no matter how correct his view is in general, he is still precisely the one who totally discredited thinking through the all too extreme form in which he defended it.

He wanted to make the significance of thoughts, of ideas really visible, by declaring the necessity in thought to be at the same time the necessity in the factual world.

One soon took his view to mean that he sought, in the world of sense-perceptible reality, even thoughts as though they were objects.

It must indeed be recognized that the field of thoughts is human consciousness alone. (SK,42)

from *The Philosophy of Freedom*

I make thinking my starting point, and not concepts and ideas which are first gained by means of thinking.

My remarks regarding the self-supporting and self-determined nature of thinking cannot, therefore, be simply transferred to concepts.

I make special mention of this, because it is here that I differ from Hegel, who regards the concept as something primary and original.[2] (PF,40)

---

2. Thus Steiner distinguishes himself from one major target of the modern aesthetic critique—Hegel being the butt of some significant anti-Romantic ideology in our own time (see, e.g. the criticism of Paul de Man).

# 5

# *On Thinking and Perception*

*We think: in every place*
*We're at the center.*

*Nature has neither core*
*Nor outer rind,*
*Being all things at once.*
*It's yourself you should scrutinize to see*
*Whether you're center or periphery.*
—Goethe, "True Enough: To the Physicist"

from *The Philosophy of Freedom*

We must next ask ourselves how … the object of observation … which meets the thinking in our consciousness, comes into our consciousness at all. (PF,43)

Our next task is to discover by means of thoughtful reflection what relation the immediately given content of observation … has to the conscious subject. (PF,44)

The failure to recognize the true relationship between mental picture and object has led to the greatest misunderstandings in modern philosophy. (PF,49)

The perception of a change in me, the modification my self undergoes, has been thrust into the foreground, while the object which causes this modification is lost sight of altogether.

It has been said that we perceive not objects but only our mental pictures.

the now predominant Kantian view … limits our knowledge of the world to our mental pictures, not because it is convinced that things cannot exist beyond these mental pictures, but because it believes us to be so organized that we can experience only the changes of our own selves, but not the things-in-themselves that cause these changes.

This view concludes from the fact that I know only my mental pictures, not that there is no reality independent of them, but only that the subject cannot directly assimilate such reality. (PF,50)

For someone who believes that the whole perceived world is only an imagined one, a mental picture, and is in fact the effect upon my soul of things unknown to me, the real problem of knowledge is naturally concerned not with the mental pictures present only in the soul but with the things which are independent of us and which lie outside our consciousness. (PF,60)

He asks: How much can we learn about these things indirectly, seeing that we cannot observe them directly? From this point of view, he is concerned not with the inner connection of his conscious percepts with one another but with their causes which transcend his consciousness and exist independently of him.

Our consciousness, on this view, works like a mirror from which the pictures of definite things disappear the moment its reflecting surface is not turned towards them.

If, now, we do not see the things themselves but only their reflections, then we must learn indirectly about the nature of the things by drawing conclusions from the behaviour of the reflections.

Modern science takes this attitude

---

The critical idealist can, however, go even further and say: I am confined to the world of my mental pictures and cannot escape from it. (PF,61)

For him there can only be two sorts of men: victims of the illusion that their own dream structures are real things, and wise men who see through the nothingness of this dream world and who must therefore gradually lose all desire to trouble themselves further about it.

Just as during sleep there appears among my dream images an image of myself, so in waking consciousness the mental picture of my own I is added to the mental picture of the outer world.

We have then given to us in consciousness, not our real I, but only our mental picture of our I.

The critical idealist then comes to the conclusion that "All reality resolves itself into a wonderful dream, without a life which the dream is about, and without a spirit which is having the dream; into a dream which hangs together in a dream of itself." (Fichte) (PF,62)

---

Whoever takes this view fails to see that there is, in fact, something which is related to mere perceiving in the way that our waking experience is related to our dreaming. This something is thinking. (PF,64)

Schopenhauer considers himself entitled … to find in the human body the "objectivity" of the will. He believes that in the activities of the body he feels an immediate reality—the thing-in-itself in the concrete.

Against these arguments it must be said that the activities of our body come to our consciousness only through percepts of the self, and that, as such, they are in no way superior to other percepts. (PF,72)

inside everything we can experience by means of perceiving, be it within ourselves or outside in the world, there is something which cannot suffer the fate of having a mental picture interpose itself between the process and the person observing it.

This something is thinking. (PF,80)

We cannot speak of anything existing beyond what is directly perceived except what can be recognized through the ideal connections of percepts, that is, connections accessible to thinking.[1]

The way objects as percepts are related to the subject as percept—a relationship that goes beyond what is merely perceived—is therefore purely ideal, that is, it can be expressed only by means of concepts. (PF,75)

---

The reason why we generally overlook thinking in our considerations of things has already been given. It lies in the fact that our attention is concentrated only on the object we are thinking about, but not at the same time on the thinking itself.

[But] [w]hat right have you to declare the world to be complete without thinking?

Set the plant before yourself. It connects itself, in your mind, with a definite concept. Why should this concept belong any less to the whole plant than leaf and blossom? (PF,65)

It is quite arbitrary to regard the sum of what we experience of a thing through bare perception as a totality, as the whole thing, while that which reveals itself through thoughtful contemplation is regarded as a mere accretion which has nothing to do with the thing itself. (PF,66)

Our whole being functions in such a way that from every real thing the relevant elements come to us from two sides, from perceiving and from thinking. (PF,67)

The separate facts appear in their true significance, both in themselves and for the rest of the world, only when thinking spins its threads from one entity to another.

The form in which this first makes its appearance we will call *intuition*.

Intuition is for thinking what observation is for the percept.

---

1.   Here we reach the essence of Steiner's view. Note how the thing-in-itself has been left behind: not so, however, the percept.

An observed object of the world remains unintelligible to us until we have within ourselves the corresponding intuition which adds that part of the reality which is lacking in the percept. (PF,73)

---

from *The Science of Knowing*

In all cognitive treatment of reality the process is as follows. We approach the concrete perception. It stands before us as a riddle. Within us the urge makes itself felt to investigate the actual what, the essential being, of the perception, which this perception itself does not express.

This urge is nothing else than a concept working its way up out of the darkness of our consciousness.[2] (SK,55)

If we therefore wish to grasp what we perceive, the perception must be prefigured in us as a definite concept. (SK,56)

from *Philosophy of Freedom*

To anyone who is incapable of finding intuitions corresponding to the things, the full reality remains inaccessible. (PF,73)

The deepening of knowledge depends on the powers of intuition which express themselves in thinking.

In the living experience which develops within thinking, this intuition may dive down to greater or lesser depths of reality.[3] (PF,107)

from *The Science of Knowing*

The only ability useful to me is one that allows a definite concept to emerge from the thought-world's supply.

---

2.    Cf. Steiner's comment on p.16 from "A thought-configuration does not come before unless I myself participate…".
3.    Note how "the living experience" has added itself to "thinking"—I comment further on this below (p.68 n.10).

The point is not that a particular thought has already become conscious for me in the course of my life, but rather that this thought allows itself to be drawn from the world of thoughts accessible to me.

It is indeed of no consequence to its content where and when I grasp it.

In fact, I draw all the characterizations of thoughts out of the world of thoughts.

Nothing whatsoever, in fact, flows into this content from the sense object.

This object does in fact move me at a particular moment to bring forth precisely this thought-content out of the unity of all possible thoughts, but it does not in any way provide me with the building-stones for these thoughts. (SK,56)

---

We are so used to seeing the world of concepts as empty and without content, and so used to contrasting perception with it as something full of content and altogether definite, that it will be difficult to establish for the world of concepts the position it deserves in the true scheme of things. (SK,57)

The concept is the single thought as it is grasped and held by the intellect.

If I bring a number of such single thoughts into living flux in such a way that they pass over into one another, connect with one another, then thought-configurations arise that are present only for the reason, that the intellect cannot attain.[4]

These configurations that reason has created shall be called *ideas* (SK,61)

Within reason, the concepts themselves combine into ideas.

a multiplicity confronts [the subjective reason] that allows itself to be led back to inner harmony. (SK,62)

---

4.   Note again "into living flux". The comment as a whole should be referred to those by Goethe above (p.26): "Theory, in and for itself, is of no use, but only inasmuch as it makes us believe in the connections of phenomena…"

if we have struggled through to where our whole thought-world bears a character of complete inner harmony, then through it the contentment our spirit demands becomes ours. Then we feel ourselves to be in possession of the truth.

[truth being nothing else than] the thorough-going harmony of all concepts we have at our command. (SK,48)

---

The fact that the idea leads a multiplicity of the concepts created by the intellect back to a unity was also expressed by Kant.

But he presented the configurations that come to manifestation through reason as mere deceptive images, as illusions that the human spirit eternally conjures up because it is eternally striving to find some unity to experience that is never to be found. (SK,61)

According to Kant, the unities created in ideas do not rest upon objective circumstances; they do not flow from the things themselves; rather they are merely subjective norms by which we bring order into our knowing.

Kant therefore does not characterize ideas as constitutive principles … but rather as regulative principles (SK,62)

---

[But, in fact] The unity that reason takes as its object is certain before all thinking

Whoever does not presuppose this must either regard all connecting of thoughts as an arbitrary activity of the subjective spirit, or he must assume that the unity stands behind the world experienced by us and compels us in some way unknown to us to lead the manifestations back to a unity.

In that case, we join thoughts without insight into the true basis of the connection that we bring about

Let us call all science taking its start from this presupposition *dogmatic*.

Every scientific view of this kind will run into difficulty when it has to give reasons for *why* we make one or another connection between thoughts. (SK,63)

Our view has shown that any assumption about some ground of being that lies outside of the idea is nonsense. (SK,72)

In thinking, postulates are not given about some ground of the world in the beyond; rather the ground of the world, in its very substance, has flowed into thinking. (SK,73)

from *The Philosophy of Freedom*

This activity of thinking is full of content.

Thinking offers this content to the percept, from man's world of concepts and ideas. (PF,73)

from *The Science of Knowing*

With thinking it is only necessary for us to overcome our own subjective limitations in order to grasp its core.

What, with the rest of reality, is factually based in the objective perception—namely, that its immediate form of appearance must be overcome in order to explain it—this, with thinking, lies only in a peculiarity of our spirit. (SK,66)

from *The Philosophy of Freedom*

If our existence were so linked up with the things that every occurrence in the world were at the same time also an occurrence in us, the distinction between ourselves and the things would not exist.

It is owing to our limitations that a thing appears to us as single and separate when in truth it is not a separate thing at all.

our understanding can grasp only single concepts out of a connected conceptual system.... due to the fact that we are not identical with the world process, but are a single being among other beings. (PF,68) [but in] thinking we have the element given to us which welds our separate individuality into one whole with the cosmos. (PF,70)

---

from *the Science of Knowing*

There is absolutely only one single thought-content, and our individual thinking is nothing more than our self, our individual personality, working its way into the thought-center of the world.[5] (SK,43)

from *The Philosophy of Freedom*

This is the deeper meaning of our two-sided nature: We see coming into being in us a force complete and absolute in itself, a force which is universal but which we learn to know, not as it issues from the centre of the world, but rather at a point in the periphery (PF,70)

Were I not a world-knower, but a world creator, object and subject (percept and I) would originate in one act. (PF,82)

Were we to know [thinking] at its source, we should understand the whole riddle of the universe the moment we became conscious.

But since we stand at a point in the periphery ... we must explore the region which lies outside our own being with the help of thinking which projects into us from the universal world existence.

The fact that thinking, in us, reaches out beyond our separate existence and relates itself to the universal world existence, gives rise to the fundamental desire for knowledge in us.

---

it is senseless to look for any common element in the separate entities of the world other than the ideal content that thinking offers us. (PF,70)

---

5.    Cf. Emerson: "In ascending to this primary and aboriginal sentiment, we have come from our remote station on the circumference instantaneously to the center of the world, where, as in the closet of God, we see causes, and anticipate the universe, which is but a slow effect." ("The Over-Soul")

All attempts to find a unity in the world other than this internally coherent ideal content, which we gain by a thoughtful contemplation of our percepts, are bound to fail.

Neither a humanly personal God, nor force, nor matter, nor the blind will (Schopenhauer) can be valid for us as a universal world unity. (PF,71)

[6]Monism never finds it necessary to ask for any principles of explanation for reality other than percepts and concepts. It knows that in the whole field of reality there is no occasion for this question. (PF,100)

Every kind of existence that is assumed outside the realm of percept and concept must be relegated to the sphere of unjustified hypotheses.

To this category belongs the 'thing-in-itself'. (PF,90)

Things demand no explanation. They exist and act on one another according to laws which can be discovered through thinking. They exist in indivisible unity with these laws.

Thus the conditions necessary for an act of knowledge to take place are there through the I and for the I.

It is not the world which sets us questions, but we ourselves.

In our knowledge we are concerned with questions which arise for us through the fact that a sphere of percepts, conditioned by place, time, and our subjective organization, is confronted by a sphere of concepts pointing to the totality of the universe.

---

6.  With the following comments Steiner distinguishes himself from virtually all Western-scientific thought up to this time, from Kant, as well as from the German romantic philosophers who, unconsciously, make as much of the things-in-themselves as Kant does.

My task consists in reconciling these two spheres, with both of which I am well-acquainted.[7]

Here one cannot speak of a limit of knowledge.

It may be that, at any particular moment, this or that remains unexplained because, through our place in life, we are prevented from perceiving the things involved. What is not found today, however, may be found tomorrow.[8] (PF,92)

The limits due to these causes are only transitory, and can be overcome by the progress of perception and thinking. (PF,93)

---

7.    It is in the sense of Steiner's argument up to this point that we should understand Owen Barfield's claim about Steiner, in *Romanticism Comes of Age* (Middletown, Connecticutt: Wesleyan University Press, 1964), namely, that if "the true *differentia* of imagination is that the subject should be somehow merged or resolved in the object" (p.30), then, "only Steiner...has clearly apprehended this activity as part, and but the first part, of a long process of *cognition* [italics mine] that may end in a man's actually overcoming the dichotomy..." (p.15)

8.    It was precisely the pretention of German romantic philosophers, in this respect, to seek to explain everything at once, before a further evolution in thought had been made (in diametric contrast, e.g., with Goethe). *Unlike* the systems of these philosophers, Coleridge's own system leaves room for this crucial fact of evolution, as we shall see below.

# 6

# *The System of Science*

from *Goethean Science*

Above all we must hold fast to the fact that the total content of science is a given one; given partly as the sense world from outside, partly as the world of ideas from within.

All our scientific activity will therefore consist in overcoming the form in which this total content of the given confronts us and in making it over into a form that satisfies us. (GS,139)

Now the methodological activity that establishes a relationship between these two forms turns out to vary according to the realm of phenomena with which we are working. (GS,140)

from *The Science of Knowing*

Nature's simplest way of working seems to us to be that in which a process results entirely from factors that confront each other externally.

It is a matter here of connecting sense-perceptible facts. (SK,75)

If the combination of facts in immediate experience does not suffice for us, then we must move on to a different combination that will satisfy our need for explanation. (SK,76)

[I explain] a complicated combination of facts by leading it back to simple facts through which, from the relationship given to the human spirit, the corresponding connection follows necessarily from the nature of the given things [e.g., the laws of trajectory, cause and effect, color etc ...] (SK,78)

Every composite process of the sense world manifests as a web of such elementary facts interpenetrated by man's spirit and can be reduced to these. (SK,79)

Such a phenoemenon ... in which the character of the process follows directly and in a transparently clear way out of the nature of the pertinent factors is called [by Goethe] an archetypal phenomenon, or a basic fact.

This archetypal phenomenon is identical with objective natural law.

We see that we can remain completely within the phenomena, and still arrive at what is necessary.

---

The inductive method adhered to so much today can never do this.
It sees a phenomenon that occurs in a particular way under the given conditions. A second time it sees the same phenomenon come about under similar conditions.

From this it infers that a general law exists according to which this event must come about, and it expresses this law as such.

Such a method remains totally outside the phenomena.

Its laws are the generalizations of individual facts.

It must always wait for confirmation of the rule by the individual facts.

*We* do not go outside the phenomenal world. (SK,80)

We place facts together in such a way that they work in accordance with their own nature, and only in accordance with it, and this working is not modified by one circumstance or another.

*Our* theory demands a definite form for every law of nature.

It presupposes a complex set of facts and determines that when this complex occurs anywhere in reality, a definite process must take place.

all laws of nature really have this form. (SK,81)

One finds that in all these individual experiences one component part remains the same. This part is higher experience within experience. It is a basic fact or archetypal phenomenon. (SK,82)

All progress in science depends upon becoming aware of archetypal phenomena. (SK,81)

———————————————

The germ of the view we have developed here is to be found in Goethe's correspondence with Schiller.

They call this method *rational empiricism*, because it takes nothing other than objective processes as content for science (SK,82)

Sense-perceptible processes in a connection with each other that can be grasped only by thinking—this is rational empiricism.[1]

———————————————

Now the sense world in its inorganic aspect ... does not show itself at any one point to be complete in itself; nowhere does there appear an individual wholeness.

In its inorganic aspect the sense world does not attain individuality.

Only in its totality is it complete in itself.

In order to have a wholeness, therefore, we must strive to grasp the entirety of the inorganic as *one* system.

Any scientific striving that does not push this far is mere preparation; it is part of the whole, not the whole itself. (SK,83)

———————————————

———————————————

1.   With the emphasis here on "connection".

from *Goethean Science*

With this, we have elaborated upon the character of inorganic nature, and have shown at the same time to what extent we can explain inorganic nature out of itself, without going out or beyond it.

No one has ever doubted this explainability, ever since one first began to think about the nature of these things. (GS,48)

But matters were different, up until Goethe, with respect to the phenomena of the *organic* world. (GS,49)

――――――――――――

[A] first view regards the finite world as a manifestation of the infinite, but this infinite remains with its own being intact; it relinquishes nothing of itself. It does not go out of itself; it remains what it was before it manifested itself.

[A] second view also regards the finite world as a manifestation of the infinite, only it assumes that this infinite, in becoming manifest, has gone entirely out of itself, has laid itself, its own being and life, into its creation in such a way that it now exists only within this creation. (GS,53)

it was readily assumed, before Goethe, with respect to inorganic nature, that one could explain it out of itself, that it carries within itself its own substantiation and essential being, but that this is not the case with organic nature.

In short: one explained organic nature according to the first view and inorganic nature according to the second. (GS,54)

――――――――――――

In the case of an organism, sense-perceptible factors appear—form, size, color, warmth, conditions of an organ, for example—that are not determined by factors of the same kind.

One cannot say of the plant, for example, that the size, form, location, etc., of the roots determine the sense-perceptible factors of the leaf or blossom.

all the sense-perceptible factors of a living being do not manifest as a result of other sense-perceptible factors, as is the case with inorganic nature.

On the contrary, in an organism, all sense-perceptible qualities manifest as the result of a factor that is no longer sense-perceptible.

we must go out of and beyond the sense world.

Observation no longer suffices (GS,49)

it is then as though we stood here before an insoluble contradiction in nature, as though a chasm existed between inorganic phenomena, which are comprehensible through themselves, and organic beings, in which an intrusion into the laws of nature occurs, in which universally valid laws seem suddenly to be broken. (GS,50)

---

from *The Science of Knowing*

For a long time science stopped short of entering the organic realm.

It believed altogether, in fact, that all lawfulness such as that at work in inorganic nature ceased here.

What was acknowledged to be the case in the inorganic world—that a phenomenon becomes comprehensible to us when we know its natural preconditions—was simply denied here.

One thought of an organism as having been purposefully constructed according to a particular design of the creator. (SK,84)

I am, after all, limited to what I have before me. If this itself does not reveal its laws to me within my thinking, then my scientific activity in fact comes to an end.

Kant, in fact, tried to establish a philosophical basis for this view.

in his view, there is a science only for the kinds of things where the particular, taken in and for itself, is entirely without concept and is only summed up under an abstract concept.

In the case of organisms Kant did not find this condition fulfilled.

Here the single phenomenon betrays a *purposeful*, i.e., a *conceptual* arrangement.

Understanding is possible for us only in the case where concept and individual thing are separated.

Thus, there is nothing left us but to base our observations about organisms upon the idea of purposefulness: to treat living beings as though a system of intentions underlay their manifestation.

Thus Kant has here established non-science scientifically, as it were. (SK,85)

---

[2]Now Goethe protested vigorously against such unscientific conduct. He could never see why our thinking should not also be adequate to ask where an organ of a living being originates instead of what purpose it serves.

For the activity of knowing the organic world, Goethe demanded a method that was scientific in exactly the same sense as the method we apply to the inorganic world. (SK,86)

Instead of investigating what it is that makes the approach to the inorganic sciences unscientific, and of then seeking a method that can be applied to the world of living things while adhering to the requirements that result from this investigation, one simply declared that the laws gained upon this lower stage of existence are universal.

[but] inorganic lawfulness is not the only one in existence but is only a special case of all possible lawfulness in general.

---

2.    What follows may well be the best defense of Goethe's scientific principles ever.

The method of physics is simply one *particular* case of a general scientific way of investigation in which the nature of the pertinent objects and the region that this science serves are taken into consideration.

If this method is extended into the organic, one obliterates the specific nature of the organic.

Instead of investigating the organic in accordance with *its* nature, one forces upon it a lawfulness alien to it. (SK,87)

------

From what do we then derive the content of that general 'something' of which we consider the individual organic entity to be a specialized case?

We know very well that the specialization comes from external influences. But we must trace the specialized shape itself back to an inner principle.

A content, configured in itself, confronts the outer phenomenal world, and this content provides us with what we need in tracing the characteristics of a particular form back to their source. (SK,89)

We must see what works in from outer circumstances as confronted by something that does not passively allow itself to be determined by them but rather determines itself, actively, out of itself, under the influence of the outer circumstances.

That basic factor is ... a general image[3] of the organism, which comprises within itself all the particular forms of organisms.[4]

Following Goethe's example, let us call this general organism the *typus*.

The typus ... is the idea of the organism: the animalness in the animal, the general plant in the specific one. (SK,90)

------

3.    Or idea.
4.    See above, p.5, from "Now, the most important thing of all was to develop this lasting, this constant element, this archetypal form with which nature, as it were, plays..."

The typus is the true archetypal organism; according to how it specializes ideally, it is either archetypal plant or archetypal animal.

The typus runs like a red thread through all the developmental stages of the organic world.

We must hold onto it and then *with* it travel through this great realm of many forms.

Then this realm will become understandable to us.

Otherwise it falls apart for us, just as the rest of the world of experience does, into an unconnected mass of particulars. (SK,91)

---

The typus … is a fuller scientific form than the archetypal phenomenon.

It presupposes a more intensive activity of our spirit than the archetypal phenomenon does.

the typus does not in fact determine the content purely formally the way a law does but rather permeates the content livingly, from within outwards, as its own.

Our spirit is confronted with the task of participating productively in the creation of the content along with the formal element.

The kind of thinking in which the content appears in direct connection with the formal element has always been called 'intuitive'. (SK,96)

We have to do here, as was expounded for the first time by Goethe, with a power to "judge in beholding".

---

Just as in organic nature the typus takes the place of the natural law (archetypal phenomenon) of inorganic nature, so intuition (the power to judge in beholding) takes the place of the proving (reflecting) power of judgment. (SK,97)

a phenomenon occurs; the conditions are there, so the phenomenon *must* occur. This is our thought process when we approach an event in the inorganic world in order to explain it. This is the method that proves things.

But we can do nothing with this proving method in organic science. (SK,95)

the typus.... offers no means of proof but can merely provide the possibility of developing every particular form out of itself. (SK,97)

The developmental method must here take the place of the proving one. (SK,95)

If an organic science wants to be a science in the sense that mechanics or physics is, it must therefore know the typus to be the most general form and must then show it also in diverse, ideal, separate shapes.

Mechanics is ... also a compilation of diverse natural laws where the real determinants are altogether hypothetically assumed. (SK,93)

in organic science.... also one would have to assume hypothetically determined forms in which the typus develops itself if one wanted to have a rational science.

One would then have to show how these hypothetical configurations can always be brought to a definite form that exists for our observation.

One can let the typus run through its series of possibilities and then always (hypothetically) hold fast to this or that form. In this way one gains a series of forms derived in thought *from* the typus, as the content of a rational organic science.[5] (SK,94)

---

*the humanities*.... demand an essentially different approach of the human spirit to its object of study than the natural sciences. (SK,101)

It is essential to the typus that it stand as something general over against its individual forms (SK,105)

---

5.   As Goethe planned this out. See above p.10 from "Then "starting at one point" to show how the archetypal organic being develops itself..."

The typus presents itself in individual forms and in these enters into interaction with the outer world.

The human spirit has only one form.

The human spirit being is not *one* configuration of its idea but rather *the* configuration of its idea.

if one wishes to attain the human spirit one must disregard the outer manifestations through which it expresses itself, disregard the specific actions it performs, and look at it in and for itself. (SK,106)

---

In our time, one has wanted to replace this method by another which considers psychology's object of study to be the phenomena in which the human spirit presents itself rather than this spirit itself.

Our study shows, however, that with this method one loses sight of the very thing that matters.

One should separate the human spirit from its various expressions and return to this spirit itself as the producer of them.

One usually limits oneself to the expressions and forgets the spirit.

Here also one has allowed oneself to be led astray, to succumb to that incorrect standpoint that wants to apply the methods of mechanics, physics, etc., to all sciences. (SK,107)

---

It is really the genuine and indeed the truest form of nature that comes to manifestation within the human spirit [i.e.,]

[not] what is brought about (the sense world) but ... what is bringing about (the inner lawfulness) (SK,101)

[Thus, if] What the human spirit can garner from the phenomena is the highest form of content that it can attain at all

[and, what's more,] If the human spirit then reflects upon itself,

[then,] it must recognize itself as the direct manifestation of this highest form

[Thus,] What the human spirit finds as unity in manifold reality it must find [identically] in the human spirit's singleness as direct existence. (SK,107)

Fichte allowed existence to the human being only insofar as he himself posits this existence within himself.

When Fichte supposed that he could found all the science of the universe upon this truth, he was in error. But it is suited to become the highest principle of *psychology*. (SK,105)

———————————————

If we succeed in discerning general laws in history, these are laws only insofar as historic personalities placed them before themselves as goals, as ideals.[6] (SK,104)

*History* is essentially a science of ideals. Its reality is, after all, ideas. (SK,113)

The ground of the world has poured itself completely out into the world; it has not withdrawn from the world in order to guide it from outside; it drives the world from inside; it has not withheld itself from the world.

The highest form in which it arises within the reality of ordinary life is thinking and, along with thinking, the human personality.

If, therefore, the world ground has goals, they are identical with the goals that the human being sets himself in living and in what he does. (SK,110)

———————————————

6.  Cf. Emerson: "the fact which is the upshot of all history [is] that there is a great responsible Thinker and Actor working wherever a man works;" ("Self-Reliance", p.26)

It is not by searching out this or that commandment of the guiding power of the world that he acts in accordance with its intentions but rather through acting in accordance with his own insights.

For within these insights[7] there lives that guiding power of the world.

It does not live as will somewhere outside the human being; it has given up all will of its own in order to make everything dependent upon man's will. (SK,110)

———————————————

But the human being does not belong only to himself; he also belongs to society.

The point is for his place within his people to be such that he can bring to full expression the strength of his individuality.

This is possible only if the social organism is such that the individual is able to find the place where he can set to work.

It must not be left to chance whether he finds his place or not. It is the task of ethnology and political science to investigate how the individual lives and acts within the social community.[8] (SK,108)

"It is not the intelligent person that rules, but rather intelligence; not the reasonable person, but rather reason," says Goethe.

To grasp the individuality of a people as a reasonable one is the method of ***ethnology***.

The human being belongs to a whole, whose nature is an organization of reason.

———————————————

7.    I.e., intuitions.
8.    Note that all begins *from* "the individual": i.e., "not the chance, single personality, not this or that personality, but rather personality as such" (SK,103); "the human spirit's singleness as direct existence"; "the human spirit reflecting upon itself" when "nature comes to manifestation" as "inner lawfulness" through thinking—in the last three cases, terms that Steiner runs through in comments quoted above (pp.50-51); or as the next quotation puts it.

Here again we can quote ... [Goethe]: "The rational world is to be regarded as a great immortal individual that unceasingly brings about the necessary, and through doing so in fact makes itself master over chance."[9] (SK,109)

---

Psychology, ethnology, and history are the major forms of the humanities.

Their methods, as we have seen, are based upon the direct apprehension of ideal reality.

The object of their study is the *idea*, the spiritual, just as the law of nature was the object of inorganic science, and the typus of organic science. (SK,113)

Man should not, like a being of inorganic nature, work upon another being in accordance with outer norms, in accordance with a lawfulness governing him;

he should also not be merely the individual form of a general typus;

rather, he should set *himself* the purpose, the goal of his existence, of his activity.

What he is in himself, what he is among his own kind, within the state and history, this he should not be through external determining factors.

How he fits himself into the structure of the world depends upon him. He must find the point where he can participate in the workings of the world.

Here the humanities receive their task. (SK,102)[10]

---

9.  And so humanity expresses itself through the psychology of peoples.
10. A task Steiner would sketch out in concrete historical detail, over thirty years later, in the "Threefold Order": see *Towards Social Renewal.*

# PART II

## The Process of Our Own Self-Consciousness

# 7

# *The Critique of Goethe*

from *Goethe's World View*

The lawfulness of nature is experienced as compelling only as long as one regards it as an alien power.

Living into its being[1], one experiences it as a power which one also exercises in one's inner life;

one experiences oneself as a productive element working along with the becoming and being of things.

One is on intimate terms with any power that has to do with becoming.

One has taken up into one's own doing what one otherwise experiences only as outer incentive.

———————————

This is the process of liberation which is effected by the act of knowledge, in the sense of the Goethean world view.

Goethe clearly perceived the ideas of nature's working as he encountered them in Italian works of art.

He had a clear experience also of the liberating effect which the possession of these ideas has upon man.

———————————

1.   For Steiner, as we have seen, a perfectly concrete experience, equivalent with 'penetrating to the idea'.

A result of this experience is his description of that kind of knowledge which he characterizes as that of encompassing individuals.

"The encompassing ones, whom one in a prouder sense could call the creative ones, conduct themselves productively in the highest sense; insofar, namely, as they take their start from ideas, they express already the unity of the whole, and afterward it is in a certain way up to nature to fit in with this idea."

But Goethe never got to the point of having a direct view of the act of liberation itself.

Goethe, to be sure, practised the highest kind of knowledge; but he did not observe this kind of knowledge in himself. (GWV,63)

Just because Goethe's thinking was consciously filled with the objects of perception, because his thinking was a perceiving, his perceiving a thinking, he could not come to the point of making thinking itself into an object of thinking.

One attains the idea of freedom, however, only by looking at thinking.

Even though the ideas *are* the content of what works within the things, they come into manifest existence through human activity. Man can therefore know the intrinsic nature of the world of ideas only if he looks at his activity.[2]

With everything else he sees he penetrates only into the idea at work in it; the thing, in which the idea works, remains as perception outside of his spirit.

When he looks at the idea, what is working and what is brought forth are both entirely contained within his inner life.

What he sees no longer appears as brought forth by the idea; for what he sees is itself now idea.

---

2.    A crucial turning point in Steiner's theory. What follows is an argument Steiner had made ten years earlier, in *The Science of Knowing*, as above pp.50-51.

In observing his thinking man sees into world happening.

Here he does not have to search after an idea of this happening, for this happening is the idea itself.

---

What one otherwise experiences as the unity of what is looked at and the ideas is here the experiencing of the spirituality of the world of ideas become visible. (GWV,64)

The person who beholds this self-sustaining activity feels freedom.

Goethe in fact experienced this feeling, but he did not express it in its highest form.

In his looking at nature he exercised a free activity, but this activity never became an object of perception for him.

He never saw behind the scenes of human knowing and therefore never took up into his consciousness the idea of world happening in its most archetypal form, in its highest metamorphosis.[3]

---

[4]As soon as a person attains a view of this metamorphosis, he then conducts himself with sureness in the realm of things.

---

3.   This critique one could extend also to the production of the English Romantic poets—to Wordsworth, Shelley, Keats—all of whom stop short at, and are principally engaged *by*, a connection to the phenomena, even when they are engaged *in* the process of imagination. The exception to this situation, as we shall see, is Coleridge who did reach down himself to the level of self-perception which Steiner sets as a standard, but who had the opposite kind of problem: that is, he could not easily find the connection to the phenomena.

     Phenomenalism is, in any case, the major limitation of *romantic* poetic (and critical) production, just as intellectualism is the major limitation of *modern* poetic (and critical) production.

     Needless to say, the path *out* of this situation was laid down by Steiner himself.

4.   Note the basis of 'certainty' in what follows.

In the center of his personality he has won the true starting point for all consideration of the world.

He will no longer search for unknown foundations, for the causes lying outside him, of things;

he knows that the highest experience of which he is capable consists of self-contemplation of his own being.

A person for whom this is not the case will seek the highest form of existence elsewhere, and, since he cannot find it within experience, will suppose it to be in an unknown region of reality.

Uncertainty will enter into his considerations of things; in answering the questions which nature poses him, he will continually call upon something he cannot investigate.

---

Because through his life in the world of ideas, Goethe had a feeling of the firm center within his personality, he succeeded, within certain limits, in arriving at sure concepts in his contemplation of nature.

But because he lacked a direct view of his innermost experiences, he groped about uncertainly outside these limits. (GWV,65)

Because Goethe did not know the innermost human experience, it was not possible for him to attain the ultimate thoughts about the moral world order which necessarily belong to his view of nature.

Whoever knows the ideas of nature only in their relation to the world we behold will also want to relate moral concepts to something external to them.

But whoever is able to view ideas in their most essential being will become aware that with moral ideas, nothing external corresponds to them, that they are directly produced as ideas in spiritual experience.

It is clear to him that neither a divine will, working only outwardly, nor a moral order of a like sort are at work to produce these ideas.

For there is in them nothing to be seen of any relation to such powers. (GWV,66)

Only through their own content do they work upon man as moral powers. (GWV,67)

this highest perception liberates man's spirit … from all one-sided feeling of dependency. (GWV,69)

---

in Goethe a feeling for the true nature of the moral held sway (GWV,67)

"Conscience needs no ancestor; with conscience everything is given;"

Other statements [however] stand in contrast to these, setting the origin of the moral into a region outside man:

"We leave to God, as the all-determining and all-liberating Being, what is totally insoluble." (GWV,68)

In his actual nature studies Goethe never speaks of unexplorable foundations, of hidden driving powers of phenomena. (GWV,71)

It is only when Goethe leaves the realm of nature that his feeling for the being of things no longer holds up.

Then his lack of human self-knowledge leads him to make assertions which are reconcilable neither with his inborn way of thinking nor with the direction of his nature studies. (GWV,72)

---

man knows the world only insofar as he knows himself. For in his inner life there reveals itself in its most archetypal form what is present to view in outer things only in reflection, in example, symbol. (GWV,68)

In every single human individuality a process occurs that plays itself out in the whole of nature: the creation of something actual out of the idea. (GWV,69)

Going beyond Goethe one must broaden his principle that nature is "great enough in the wealth of its creation to make, after thousandfold plants, one in which all the others are contained, and to make, after thousandfold animals, one being that contains them all: man."

Nature is so great in its creation that it repeats in every human individual the process by which it brings forth freely out of the idea all creatures, repeats it through the fact that moral actions spring from the ideal foundation of the personality.

for there dwells in my inner life in an individual form the working power by which nature creates the universe.[5]

As long as a person has not beheld this working power within himself, he will appear with respect to it the way Faust did with respect to the earth spirit.

This working power will always call out to him the words: "You resemble the spirit that you can grasp, not me!"

Only the beholding of one's deepest inner life conjures up this spirit; who says of itself:

In the tides of life, in action's storm,
Up and down I wave,
To and fro weave free,
Birth and the grave,
An infinite sea,
A varied weaving,
A radiant living,
Thus at Time's humming loom it's my hand that prepares

---

5.    Here we have worked our way up "from the product to the production" (see above p.17); here we "make ourselves worthy, through beholding an ever-creating nature, of participating spiritually in its productions." (p.21). Cf. Emerson: "For the sense of being which in calm hours rises, we know not how, in the soul, is not diverse from the things…but one with them, and proceeds obviously from the same source whence their life and being also proceed. We first share the life by which things exist, and afterwards see them as appearances in nature, and forget we have shared their cause." ("Self-Reliance")

The robe ever-living the Deity wears. (GWV,70)

---

I have tried to present in my *Philosophy of Spiritual Activity*[6] how knowledge of the fact that man in his doing is based upon himself comes from the most inward experience, from the beholding of his own being.

Goethe did not go so far as to behold freedom, because he had an antipathy for self-knowledge.[7]

If that had not been the case, then knowledge of man as a free personality founded upon himself would have had to be the peak of his world view.

The germ of this knowledge is to be found everywhere in his works; (GWV,71)

from *The Philosophy of Freedom*

For everyone, however, who has the ability to observe thinking—and with good will every normal man has this ability—this observation is the most important one he can possibly make.

For he observes something of which he himself is the creator; he finds himself confronted not by an apparently foreign object but by his own activity. (PF,29)

My investigation touches firm ground only when I find an object which exists in a sense which I can derive from the object itself. But I am myself such an object in that I think, for I give to my existence the definite self-determined content of the thinking activity. (PF,30)

---

6.    An alternative title for *The Philosophy of Freedom*.
7.    Steiner quotes Goethe himself: "I hereby confess that from the beginning the great and significant sounding task—know thou thyself, has always seemed suspect to me, as a ruse of secretly united priests who wanted to confuse man with unattainable demands and to seduce him away from activity in the outer world into an inner false contemplation. Man knows himself only insofar as he knows the world, which he becomes aware of only within himself and himself only within it. Every new object which we really look at opens up a new organ within us."
    Steiner comments on this: "Exactly the reverse of this is true: man knows the world only insofar as he knows himself." (See *Goethe's World View*, p.68)

the point that matters is that nothing is willed which, in being carried out, does not appear to the 'I' as an activity completely its own and under its own supervision. (PF,38)

# 8

# *Coleridge and Romantic Theory*

from Coleridge's *Biographia Literaria*
(Chapters Twelve and Thirteen)

[1]They and they only can acquire the philosophic imagination, the sacred power of self-intuition, who within themselves can interpret and understand the symbol, that the wings of the air-sylph are forming within the skin of the caterpillar; those only, who feel in their own spirits the same instinct, which impels the chrysallis of the horned fly to leave room in its involucrum for antennae yet to come.

They know and feel that the potential works *in* them[2], even as the actual works *on* them. (BL,236)

On the immediate which dwells in every man, and on the original intuition, or absolute affirmation of it (which is likewise in every man, but does not in every man rise to consciousness), all the certainty of our knowledge depends. (BL,237)

Only in the self-consciousness of a spirit is there the required identity of object and of representation; for therein consists the essence of a spirit, that it is self-representative.

---

1.  Coleridge's discourse in what follows is identical with Steiner's. The reader will thus recognize the value of Coleridge's discourse as a condensation and distillation of what precedes. The same is true of the writings of Emerson, the great representative of Romantic theory in America, the symmetry of whose thoughts with Steiner's extends still further—see, e.g., Emerson's "Nature", "Self-Reliance", "History", "The Over Soul". It should be obvious that in elaborating his views, Steiner was not working either from Coleridge or from Emerson.
2.  *In the encounter with* the actual.

If, therefore, this be the one, only immediate truth, in the certainty of which the reality of our collective knowledge is grounded, it must follow that the spirit in all objects which it views views only itself. (BL,250)

The necessary tendence therefore of all natural philosophy is from nature to intelligence; and this, and no other, is the true ground and occasion of the instinctive striving to introduce theory into our views of natural phaenomena.

The highest perfection of natural philosophy would consist in the perfect spiritualization of all the laws of nature into laws of intuition and intellect. The phaenomena (the material) must wholly disappear, and the laws alone (the formal) must remain.

Thence it comes, that in nature itself the more the principle of law breaks forth, the more does the husk drop off, the phaenomena themselves become more spiritual and at length cease altogether in our consciousness. (BL,243)

[3]Again, the spirit (originally the identity of object and subject[4]) must in some sense *dissolve* this identity, in order to be conscious of it

But this implies an act, and it follows therefore that intelligence or self-consciousness is impossible, except by and in a will.[5]

The self-conscious spirit therefore is a will; and freedom must be assumed as a *ground* of philosophy, and can never be deduced from it.[6]

---

3.    With the following formulations, we reach the very heart of English romantic theory; they were to constitute, unconsciously and half-consciously, the theoretical formulation of much later imaginative writing in criticism. We note especially Coleridge's emphasis on the imagination as act of will. However, in his own and later criticism, the effort of will (or the understanding of it) did not go far enough—as I argue in *Othello's Sacrifice* (Part Three).

4.    I.e., object and subject in a state of *un*differentiation.

5.    Cf. Steiner: *The Philosophy of Freedom*: "the free act of will consists in the fact that, firstly, through the intuitive element, the activity that is necessary for the human organism is checked and repressed, and then replaced by the spiritual activity of the idea-filled will...man is unfree insofar as he cannot complete the process of suppressing the organic activity." (p.173)

6.    See below (p.74) for Steiner's elaborations of this.

This *principium commune essendi et cognoscendi,* as subsisting in a will, or primary act of self-duplication, is the mediate or indirect principle of every science; but it is the immediate or direct principle of the ultimate science alone, i.e., of transcendental philosophy alone. (BL,250)

In its very idea as a systematic knowledge of our collective knowing (*scientia scientiae*) it involves the necessity of some highest principle of knowing, as at once the source and accompanying form in all particular acts of intellect and perception. This, it has been shown, can be found only in the act and evolution of self-consciousness.[7]

We are not investigating an absolute *principium essendi;* for then, I admit, many valid objections might be started against our theory; but an absolute *principium cognoscendi.*[8]

It is asserted only, that the act of self-consciousness is for us the source and principle of all *our* possible knowledge.

Whether abstracted from us there exists any thing higher and beyond this primary self-knowing, which is for us the form of all our knowing, must be decided by the result.[9]

in short, that self-consciousness may be itself something explicable into something which must lie beyond the possibility of our knowledge, because the whole

---

7.  Note the further emphasis, after the "act", on "evolution".
8.  In deferring to the idea of an "absolute principium <u>essendi</u>", Coleridge associates himself with the project of the German romantic philosophers, notably Schelling. Much of the material from these two chapters of the *Biographia* is developed around an idea, derived from Schelling, of the absolute identity of Subject and Object. From this idea Coleridge, it would appear, felt obliged to begin. However, Coleridge's <u>other</u> focus, on an "absolute principium <u>cognoscendi</u>", directly contradicts the first approach, and is Coleridge's own. It is the project with which Coleridge clearly wished to associate himself. The following comments by Coleridge highlight the difference between the two positions.
9.  See p.40 n.8.

synthesis of our intelligence is first formed in and through the self-consciousness, does not at all concern us as transcendental philosophers.

for us, self-consciousness is not a kind of being, but a king of knowing, and that too the highest and farthest that exists for us.

even when the Objective is assumed as the first, we yet can never pass beyond the principle of self-consciousness.

Should we attempt it, we must be driven back from ground to ground, each of which would cease to be a ground the moment we pressed on it. (BL,251)

---

[10]Bearing then this in mind, that intelligence is a self-development, not a quality supervening to a substance, we may abstract from all degree, and for the purpose of philosophic construction reduce it to kind, under the idea of an indestructible power with two opposite and counteracting forces.

The intelligence in the one tends to *objectize* itself[11], and in the other to *know* itself in the object.

It will be hereafter my business to construct by a series of intuitions the progressive schemes, that must follow from such a power with such forces, till I arrive at the fullness of the *human* intelligence. (BL,252)

When we have formed a scheme or outline of these two different kinds of force, and of their different results by the process of discursive reasoning, it will then remain for us to elevate the thesis from notional to actual—by contemplating intuitively this one power with its two inherent, indestructible yet counteracting

---

10.   Like Steiner (and Goethe), Coleridge assumes a power of thinking and knowledge that emerges from experience or nature. Having dwelt on thinking as one associated element, Coleridge now restores the other element of experience or nature to view. Hence, the distinction below between "the living principle" (i.e., nature), and "the process of self-consciousness" (i.e., thinking or knowledge). Consider how every so often Steiner himself stops to acknowledge the other element that is always implied. See, e.g., p.34 n.3 and p.35 n.4.
11.   I.e., after dissolution.

forces, and the results or generations to which their interpenetration gives exist-ence, *in the living principle and in the process of our own self-consciousness.* (BL,260)

[12]the transcendental philosopher says; grant me a nature having two contrary forces, the one of which tends to expand infinitely, while the other strives to apprehend or *find* itself in this infinity, and I will cause the world of intelligences with the whole system of their representations to rise up before you.[13] (BL,258)

For my present purpose, I *assume* such a power as my principle, in order to deduce from it ... (BL,252)

the nature and genesis of the imagination (BL,256)

The ... imagination I consider as ... co-existing with the conscious will ... It *dis-solves*, diffuses, dissipates, in order to re-create; or where this process is rendered impossible, yet still at all events it struggles to idealize and to unify. (BL,263)

([cf.] Again, the spirit (originally the identity of object and subject) must in some sense *dissolve* this identity, in order to be conscious of it ... this implies an act, and it follows therefore that intelligence or self-consciousness is impossible, except by and in a will.... and freedom must be assumed (BL,250))

---

12.  Note how the scheme is now centered in "nature".
13.  "one of which tends to expand infinitely": the process of 'objectizing'/'objectifica-tion' is thus 'infinite'.

   And as we come to discover, as romantic readers, 'expansion' is *in* the 'soul-object', since "the soul", as Schlegel put it (in *The Philosophy of Life*), "*is* the life of nature".

   It is, at the same time, always 'expansion' in 'the whole', i.e., in the 'idea', and "the great [spiritual] whole that the idea encompasses" (see p.18). Thus, nature "strives to apprehend or find itself in this infinity" in the *idea* that is potentially avail-able to man.

   ...'expansion' in the soul-object'/'expansion in the idea': Steiner's later presenta-tion of spiritual facts builds continually on this double experience, simply because it is the principle underlying the evolution of all created existence. See, e.g., Steiner's *Genesis*, pp.15-16.

   We need to recall, also, that 'expansion' itself depends on a prior process of 'dis-solution'. This is made clear (again) in what Coleridge says about the 'Imagination' in what follows.

from Steiner's *The Philosophy of Freedom*

Our next task must be to define the concept of 'mental picture' more closely. (PF,77)

The moment a percept appears in my field of observation, thinking also becomes active through me. An element of my thought system, a definite intuition, a concept connects itself with the percept.

Then, when the percept disappears from my field of vision, what remains? My intuition, with the reference to the particular percept which it acquired in the moment of perceiving.

A mental picture is nothing but an intuition related to a particular percept; it is a concept that was once connected with a certain percept, and which retains the reference to this percept.

Thus the mental picture is an individualized concept. (PF,84)

The sum of those things about which I can form mental pictures may be called my total *experience*. The man who has the greater number of individualized concepts will be the man of richer experience. (PF,85)

---

However, we are not satisfied merely to refer the percept, by means of thinking, to the concept, but we relate them also to our particular subjectivity, our individual Ego.[14]

Our thinking links us to the world; our feeling leads us back into ourselves and thus makes us individuals.

---

14.  From here Steiner's account of thinking is related to the total experience of the individual as this includes feeling and willing. The problems of late nineteenth century romantic 'experience' are addressed in so far as it shows a marked tendency to develop in one direction or the other, without the central reference to thinking. In either case, it was a matter of mistaking the percept for the whole, which can only be found in the idea.

It is only because we experience self-feeling with self-knowledge, and pleasure and pain with the perception of objects, that we live as individual beings whose existence is not limited to the conceptual relations between us and the rest of the world, but who have besides this a special value for ourselves. (PF,86)

---

Thinking, therefore, reveals itself in the percept of the self. (PF,113)

This relationship in thought of the self to itself is what, in life, determines our personality.

This determination of our life would remain a purely conceptual (logical) one, if no other determinations of our self were added to it.

We should then be creatures whose life was expended in establishing purely ideal relationships between percepts among themselves and between them and ourselves.

[But we] relate percepts to ourselves not merely ideally, through concepts, but also ... through feeling.

---

[But to] begin with feeling is exactly the same, on the subjective side, as the percept is on the objective side. (PF,114)

For the universe as a whole my life of feeling can have value only if, as a percept of myself, the feeling enters into connection with a concept and in this round-about way links itself to the cosmos. (PF,86)

A true individuality will be the one who reaches up with his feelings to the farthest possible extent into the region of the ideal. (PF,86)

Monism ... must grant the same addition to feeling that it considers necessary for percepts, if these are to stand before us in full reality.

for monism, feeling is an incomplete reality, which, in the form in which it first appears to us, does not yet contain its second factor, the concept or idea. (PF,114)

However, what for us appears only later, is from the first indissolubly bound up with our feeling.

This is why the naïve man comes to believe that in feeling he is presented with existence directly, in knowledge only indirectly.

The tendency just described, the philosophy of feeling, is often called *mysticism*.

The error in a mystical outlook based upon mere feeling is that it wants to experience directly what it ought to gain through knowledge; that it wants to raise feeling which is individual, into a universal principle. (PF,115)

---

In feeling [the I] has direct experience of a relation of the objects to itself as subject. In the will, the case is reversed.

In willing, we are concerned once more with a percept, namely, that of the individual relation of our self to what is objective.

Whatever there is in willing that is not a purely ideal factor, is just as much mere object of perception as is any object in the external world.

Nevertheless, the naïve realist believes here again that he has before him something far more real than can be attained by thinking. (PF,116)

The philosophy of will [*thelism*] turns into metaphysical realism when it places the element of will even into those spheres of existence where it cannot be experienced directly, as it can in the individual subject.[15]

It assumes, outside the subject, a hypothetical principle for whose real existence the sole criterion is subjective experience.

As a form of metaphysical realism, the philosophy of will ... has to get over [itself] ... and ... acknowledge that the will is a universal world process only in so far as it is ideally related to the rest of the world. (PF,117)

---

15.   E.g., Schopenhauer.

Thinking all too readily leaves us cold in recollection; it is as if the life of the soul had dried out. Yet this is really nothing but the strongly marked shadow of its real nature—warm, luminous, and penetrating deeply into the phenomena of the world.

This penetration is brought about by a power flowing through the activity of thinking itself—the power of love in its spiritual form. (PF,119)

If we turn towards thinking in its essence, we find in *it* both feeling and will, and these in the depths of their reality; if we turn away from thinking towards 'mere' feeling and will, we lose from these their true reality. (PF,120)

There are no grounds here for the objection that to discern love in the activity of thinking is to project into thinking a feeling, namely, love. For in truth, this objection is but a confirmation of what we have been saying. (PF,119)

The highest level of individual life is that of conceptual thinking without regard to any definite perceptual content. We determine the content of a concept through pure intuition from out of the ideal sphere.

But if we act under the influence of intuitions, the driving force of our action is pure thinking. As it is the custom in philosophy to call the faculty of pure thinking 'reason', we may well be justified in giving the name of *practical reason* to the moral driving force characteristic of this level of life. (PF,128)

Among the levels of characterological disposition, we have singled out as the highest the one that works as pure thinking or practical reason. Among the motives, we have singled out *conceptual intuition* as the highest. (PF,132)

Insofar as this intuitive content applies to action, it constitutes the moral content of the individual.[16]

To let this content express itself in life is both the highest moral driving force and the highest motive a man can have, who sees that in this content all other moral principles are in the end united. We may call this point of view *ethical individualism*.[17] (PF,134)

---

I act, at this level of morality, not because I acknowledge a lord over me, or an external authority, or a so-called inner voice; I acknowledge no external principle for my action, because I have found in myself the ground for my action, namely, my love of the action. (PF,135)

If we want to understand the nature of the human will, we must distinguish between the path which leads this will to a certain degree of development and the unique character which the will assumes as it approaches this goal. (PF,136)

Our life is made up of free and unfree actions.

We cannot, however, think out the concept of man completely without coming upon the *free spirit* as the purest expression of human nature. (PF,140)

Man must unite his concept with the percept of man by his own activity.

This he can do only if he has found the concept of the free spirit, that is, if he has found the concept of his own self. (PF,141)

Monism, then, in the sphere of true moral action, is a freedom philosophy. (PF,151)

---

16.  Cf. Novalis's "ethical grace": "If I could only ignite this love for the ethical grace (Grazie), for the moral beauty, into the purest, most noble passion which has ever permeated a mortal bosom with its fiery glow!" (cited by William Lindeman, ed., and tr., *Spiritual Songs* (Spring Valley, N.Y.: Mercury Press, 1986), p.27.

17.  Whose expression is 'moral imagination' (a subject Steiner also addresses in *The Philosophy of Freedom*).

In the objective world a dividing line is drawn by our organization between percept and concept; knowledge overcomes this division.

In our subjective nature this division is no less present; man overcomes it in the course of his development by bringing the concept of himself to expression in his outward existence.

Hence, not only man's intellectual life but also his moral life leads to his twofold nature, perceiving (direct experience) and thinking.

The intellectual life overcomes this twofold nature by means of knowledge, the moral life overcomes it through the actual realization of the free spirit. (PF,141)

# 9

# *Knowledge of the Higher Worlds*

*Action eternal, vivid, rose;*
*And what was not, now wishes to unfold …*

*Soul of the world, soak into us, descend,*
*Then with the very* <u>Weltgeist</u> *to contend*
*Our finest faculties contract;*
*Spirits benign will guide and sympathize,*
*Sublimest masters gently ways devise*
*To the perpetual Creative Act.*

—Goethe, "One and All"

from Steiner's *Philosophy of Freedom*

This book aims at presenting no more than can be surveyed through the experience of intuitive thinking.

Whatever comes to us by way of percept is something that, on our journey through life, we simply have to await.

The only question is would it be right to expect, from the point of view that this purely intuitively experienced thinking gives us, that man could perceive spiritual things as well as those perceived with the senses.[1] (PF,220)

---

1.  Here Steiner pursues his view in the direction Coleridge himself would have wished to but dare not in his own time simply because in the whole of England he would have been working alone in this direction. (Coleridge abandoned his speculations at the point we have covered.)

It would be right to expect this. For, although on the one hand, intuitively experienced thinking is an active process taking place in the human spirit, on the other hand, it is also a spiritual percept grasped without a physical sense organ.

It is a percept in which the perceiver is himself active, and a self-activity which is at the same time perceived.

In intuitively experienced thinking man is carried into a spiritual world as perceiver. (PF,221)

---

From *Goethe's World View*

It lies in the sense of the Goethean world view first of all to provide knowing with a firm basis through the fact that the world of ideas, in its essential being, is seen connected with nature, in order then, within the world of ideas thus consolidated, to advance to an experience beyond the sense world.[2]

Even then, when regions are known which do not lie in the realm of the sense world, one's gaze is still directed towards the living harmony of idea and experience, and certainty of knowledge is sought thereby. (GWV,30)

from *The Philosophy of Freedom*

Within this spiritual world, whatever confronts him as percept in the same way that the spiritual world of his own thinking does will be recognized by him as a world of spiritual perception.

*This* world of spiritual perception could be seen as having the same relationship to thinking that the world of sense perception has on the side of the senses.

Such a world of spiritual perception is discussed in a number of writings which I have published since [*The Philosophy of Freedom*] first appeared. (PF,221)

---

2.    Here we may identify the chief project of the great Romantic poets: Coleridge, Wordsworth, Shelley, Keats, Novalis etc...However, only Coleridge and Novalis would seem to have fully *understood* what this project entailed. See pp.66-67 above; also p.83 n.8.

from Steiner's *Christianity as Mystical Fact*

[But] the presentation of a spiritual fact ... can only be recognized in its true nature by a cognition derived from the sources of spiritual life itself. (CMF,vii)

---

from Steiner's *Knowledge of the Higher Worlds*

there is ... no difference between occult knowledge and the rest of man's knowledge (KHW,20)

from *Christianity as Mystical Fact*

We shall ... apply to the higher regions of spiritual life the methods ... used in the study of nature. (CMF,7)

from Steiner's *Theosophy*

The author ... describes nothing to which he cannot bear witness from *experience*—the kind of experience that belongs to [supersensible] regions. (TH,viii)

---

People will certainly be prone to demand that he give irrefutable proofs for what he states, but they do not realize that in doing so, they are victims of a misconception.

They demand ... not the proofs lying within the things themselves, but those that they personally are willing to recognize or are in a condition to recognize. (TH,xi)

---

from Steiner's *Science of Knowing*

One must bear in mind that intuition means something completely different within *our* scientific direction—which is convinced that in thinking we grasp the core of the world in its essential being

A person who sees in the world lying before us … nothing more than a reflection (an image of some other-worldly, unknown, active principle that remains hidden behind this shell not only to one's first glance but also to all scientific investigation) such a person can certainly regard the proving method as nothing but a substitute for the insight we lack into the essential being of things. (SK,98)

Since he does not press through to the view that a thought-connection comes about directly through the *essential* content given in thought, i.e., through the thing itself, he believes himself able to support this thought-connection only through the fact that it is in harmony with several basic convictions (axioms) so simple that they are neither susceptible of proof nor in need thereof.

If such a person is then presented with a scientific statement without proof, a statement, indeed, that by its very nature excludes the proving method, then it seems to him to be imposed from outside. A truth approaches him without his knowing what the basis of its validity is.

He believes he has no knowledge, no insight into the matter; he believes he can only give himself over to the faith that, *outside his powers of thought*, some basis or other for its validity exists.

Our world view is in no danger of having to regard the limits of the proving method as at the same time the limits of scientific conviction.

With intuition a truth is not imposed upon us from outside, because, from our standpoint, there *is* no inner and outer in the sense assumed by the scientific direction just characterized and that is in opposition to our own.

For us, intuition is a direct being-within, a penetrating into the truth that gives us everything that pertains to it at all. (SK,99)

It merges completely with what is given to us in our intuitive judgment.

The essential characteristic of *faith* is totally absent here (SK,100)

---

from *Theosophy*

It is not, however, only to researchers into the spiritual world that the observer of the supersensible has to speak. (TH,xviii)

even those who are still far from the moment in which they will acquire the ability to make their own spiritual research can bring a measure of understanding to meet him. (TH,xix)

from *Christianity as Mystical Fact*

Today spiritual knowledge can be conceptually understood, because in more recent times man has acquired a conceptual capacity that formerly was lacking.

Nowadays some people can have cognition of the spiritual world through their own experiences, and others can understand such experiences conceptually. (CMF,20)

from *Theosophy*

Certain powers are required to discover the things referred to, but if after having been discovered they are made known, every person can understand them who is willing to bring to them unprejudiced logic and a healthy sense of truth.

the things made known are wholly of a kind that must produce the impression that through them the riddles of human life and the phenomena of the world can be satisfactorily approached. (TH,xx)

This impression will be produced upon everyone who permits thought, unclouded by prejudice, and a feeling for truth free and without reservation, to work within him. (TH,xxi)

---

[3][The observer of the supersensible] addresses himself first to this understanding that can flash forth in every human soul.

He knows that in this understanding there is a force that must slowly lead to the higher degrees of knowledge.

---

3.    Here then is the justification of a relation of supersensible experience.

This feeling which perhaps at first perceives nothing at all of what it is told, is itself the magician that opens the 'eye of the spirit'.

In darkness this feeling stirs. The soul sees nothing, but through this feeling it is seized by the power of truth.

The truth then gradually draws nearer to the soul and opens the higher sense in it. (TH,xix)

------

We ought not to doubt for one moment the possibility of opening the eyes of every earnest person to these things.

On this supposition all those have written and spoken who have felt within themselves that the inner sense-instrument had developed, enabling them to know the true nature and being of man

Hence from the most ancient times such a *hidden wisdom* has been spoken of again and again. (TH,xviii)

The wisdom ... that ... reveals [to man] ... his own being and with it his final goal, may well be called *divine wisdom* or *theosophy*.

To the study of the spiritual processes in human life and in the cosmos, the term *spiritual science* may be given.

When ... one extracts from this spiritual science those special results that have reference to the spiritual *core* of man's being, then the expression *theosophy* may be employed to designate this domain because it has been employed for centuries in this way. (TH,xxii)[4]

------

from *Knowledge of the Higher Worlds*[5]

------

4.   *Theo*sophy becomes in our time *Anthropo*sophy inasmuch as the whole evolution of our cosmos is now centred in man.

In every human being there slumber faculties by means of which he can acquire for himself a knowledge of higher worlds.

It can only be a matter of how to set to work to develop such faculties.[6]

As long as a human race has existed there has always been training, in the course of which individuals possessed of the higher faculties gave audience to those who were seeking for them. (KHW,19)

a certain fundamental attitude of the soul must be the starting-point.

prepare in your soul a worthy reception[7]

the spiritual investigator calls this the path of veneration—devotion to truth and knowledge (KHW,22)

we must develop in ourselves the deeply rooted feeling that there is something higher than ourselves[8] (KHW,23)

every feeling of true devotion harboured in the soul develops a power which leads sooner or later to a further stage of knowledge.

---

5.    Note that in the pages that follow I have proceeded through a free transcription of many of the texts linked to *Knowledge of the Higher Worlds* that focus on a meditative practice. To facilitate the reader's concentration I have dispensed with all elaborate symbolical notations indicating jumps in the text, insertions etc.., all of which would have greatly encumbered reading. In what follows I therefore offer texts in which Steiner's phrasing of ideas is shaped by my own structural presentation.

6.    It is in this respect that Steiner distinguishes himself from every Romantic theorist before or after him: his 'theory' is, at the same time, a 'path' of knowledge minutely outlined for all to pursue, and so, the basis for 'culture'.

7.    In the "soul" for, as Steiner remarks below, "it is the soul that exercises cognition". Cf. Emerson: "Meantime within man is the soul of the whole"; "All goes to show that the soul in man is not an organ, but animates and exercises all the organs; is not a function, like the power of memory, of calculation...; is not a faculty, but a light; is not the intellect or the will, but the master of the intellect and the will; is the background of our being in which they lie—"; "For the Maker of all things and all persons stands behind us, and casts his dread omniscience through us over things." "From within or from behind, a light shines through us upon things, and makes us aware that we are nothing, but the light is all." (From "The Over-Soul").

the pupil undertakes by a rigourous self-education to engender within himself this attitude of devotion (KHW,24)

this cannot be done through study

everywhere he must look for whatever can capture his admiration and respect (KHW,25)

enter lovingly into the qualities of another

look for the good in all things

to discover what remains in our consciousness of adverse judgments brings us nearer to higher knowledge (KHW,26)

man begins to see things which he had been unable to see (KHW,27)

---

8.   "Indeed", says Rudolf Steiner, "it is always this wonder and this astonishment which guide us to the supersensible, and it is at the same time also that quality which one usually calls faith". "In our soul we must have what enables us to look towards a supersensible world, what can direct all our thoughts and ideas towards such a world". "We have also pointed out that the capacities of human beings will be enhanced..." (cited by Sergei O. Prokofieff in *Eternal Individuality* (London: Temple Lodge, 1987), pp.119-120).

Prokofieff adds: "Novalis, too, knows of this future transition of the power of faith into the forces of higher supersensible vision...connected with the extraordinary development in the modern world of the forces of the intellect...*[T]he power of faith within the human soul is strengthened to such a degree that in its yearning for the supersensible it is also able—so to speak—to embrace the intellectual principle* [italics mine]....However, this will be possible only when the power of faith...*is permeated by a real moral will* [italics mine]. For only a faith which is permeated by a will that strives towards higher knowledge is capable of transforming the modern intellect into a new capacity of conscious clairvoyance..." (pp.120-121)

For the sense of 'will' in this context, cf. Coleridge above pp.66-67.

"Novalis, too, refers...to such a transformation of the intellectual forces: "*In the will is the ground of creation. Faith is the effect of the will upon the intellect...*"" (p.122, italics mine)

In another context, Novalis calls this "the true divination sense", Kluckhohn, III,250, cited by William Lindeman, *Op. cit.,* p.22.

we draw towards us qualities in the beings around us previously concealed (KHW,28)

but transformation must take place in his inmost self, in his life of thought (KHW,26)

the life of soul finds it centre in reverence for everything truly venerable (KHW,27)

for it is the soul that exercises cognition (KHW,28)

———————————————

[9]develop an active inner life (KHW,28)

allow what one has experienced of the outer world to echo (KHW,29)

enjoyment is allowed to *reveal* something

is renounced, worked over inwardly (KHW,30)

to be placed in the service of the world

thus every idea becomes an ideal, engendering life-forces (KHW,31)

———————————————

provide for moments of inner tranquility (KHW,32)

moments of seclusion (KHW,33)

look at everything from a higher standpoint[10]

we contemplate and judge our experiences and actions as though they were those of others

———————————————

9.    To a first idea of 'devotion' is now added the idea of 'work'.
10.   'Detachment'.

the pupil stands towards himself as a stranger, with the inner calmness of a judge

---

while entangled, we are connected with the non-essential (KHW,34)

[now] the essential separates from the non-essential

we survey the whole at once

proportions appear different (KHW,35)

the pupil is acquiring a 'higher' life (KHW,36)

the higher man is awakening[11] (KHW,35)

he will become more serene ... no longer disconcerted, angered, alarmed, anxious ... more and more his guide

"I will do my work as well as I possibly can" (KHW,36)

thus thought after thought, fruitful, beneficial, flow into the pupil's outlook

calmness and certainty bring about the growth of the inner man, and with the inner man faculties which lead to higher knowledge

he is able to take from a word its wounding or vexing sting (KHW,37)

impatience vanishes replaced by worthwhile observation

---

the 'higher' man is in constant development

---

11. Here, we might say, is where the process of 'expansion' begins—after 'dissolution'. 'Dissolution' is reflected to us in 'work', 'detachment' (Cf. Steiner's *Leading Thoughts*: "the Thinking that is stimulated from without must be taken hold of inwardly, and experienced as such, intensely in the soul, apart from its relation to the outer world." (p.17))

In a subsequent stage, the latter experience ('detachment') intensifies to 'concentration', in which 'expansion' or 'meditation' proceeds.

only tranquility and certainty make his orderly and regular development possible. This higher man becomes the 'inner ruler' who directs the circumstances of the outer man; impressions approach me in a way I myself determine (KHW,38)

everything depends on the pupil confronting himself as a complete stranger, but only one side of the pupil's inner activity is characterized by this birth of the 'higher' man[12]

the pupil, must now rise to the purely human reality

he must pass on to the contemplation of those things that would concern him as a man if he lived under quite different conditions and in a quite different situation

In this way something begins to live within him which transcends the personal (KHW,39)

he begins to realize as actual experience that he belongs to 'higher worlds'.

he moves the central point of his being into his inner nature.

calm inner contemplation and converse with the purely spiritual world fill his whole soul

he is completely absorbed in a world of thought[13]

[the pupil] must develop a living feeling for this silent thought-activity

must learn to love the inflow of the spirit

life expresses itself in this thought world (KHW,40)

---

12.   This 'birth of a higher man' corresponds to Coleridge's focus on that force of 'nature' in us that "expands infinitely" (see p.69)—i.e., the 'soul'. This 'birth' is now counterbalanced in Steiner's account by that 'other' force of nature which "strives to apprehend or find itself in this infinity"—i.e., 'the thinking spirit'.

the life of the soul in thought widens into a life in the spiritual reality of being (KHW,41)

---

where human nature is united with the spirit, the eternal is kindled to life

meditation leads man to knowledge and vision of the eternal indestructible core of his being (KHW,43)

from Steiner's *Occult Science*

---

13.   Cf. Steiner: "It is of greatest importance that the student of the spiritual has acquired a quite <u>definite</u> soul state when he becomes conscious of a new-born ego. For through his ego the human being attains to control of his sensations, feelings, thoughts, instincts, passions, and desires. Perception and thought cannot be left to themselves in the soul. They must be regulated through attentive thinking. It is the ego that employs these laws of thinking and through them brings order into the life of visualization and thought." (from *Occult Science*, p.281)

   This is 'concentration': i.e., the act and activity of self-consciousness that emerges in and from 'dissolution' (in another context, Steiner refers to this activity as "pure love of the action").

   See also Steiner, *Leading Thoughts*: "When for an experience in consciousness a process of disintegration has taken place, that which has been demolished will be built up again exactly. The experience of Self-consciousness lies in the perception of this upbuilding process. The same process can be observed with inner vision. We then feel how the Conscious is led over into the Self-conscious by man's *creating out of himself* an after-image of the merely Conscious."

   "The Thinking which has become alive in meditation must now be permeated by the Will.... What we thus called to life in our consciousness by a more passive devotion must now be *reproduced* by ourselves, by an act of will." (p.18)

   Cf. Coleridge on "self-duplication" above, pp.66-67.

   Steiner could also see a development in higher knowledge from its end point or 'other' side: see, e.g., his *Leading Thoughts*, pp.92-93: "in the consciousness there are the forces which represent the life of the Ego in freedom. For the inward perception of man himself there is the consciousness of his activity in freedom, but for the Spiritual Beings connected with man from other spheres of the Universe it is different"; "they see, how...cosmic forces...want to form and mould him further—"; "bringing...to man from the spiritual part of the Cosmos forces which can replace those from the realm of Nature which have been suppressed."

This is the first purely spiritual experience: the observation of a soul-spirit ego being. This, as a new self, has lifted itself out of the self that is only bound to the physical senses and the physical intellect.

The soul-spiritual being, naturally, existed before meditation had taken place, but it did not yet have any organs for observing the spiritual world.

The force that was employed in meditation first has fashioned the soul-spirit organs out of the previously unorganized soul-spirit nature. (OS,274)

---

from *Knowledge of the Higher Worlds*

Spiritual Science offers the means whereby the spiritual ears and eyes are developed[14] (KHW,43)

the 'body' of soul and spirit is equipped with higher 'senses' through a definite cultivation of the life of feeling and thought

PREPARATION

---

A.
direct the attention of the soul to phenomena of budding, growing ... fading, decay (KHW,46)

observing growth, a man must banish everything else from the soul

give yourself up to the feeling and the thought arising in the soul

feeling now acquires a strong and energetic form

the more often attention is turned upon something that is growing and then upon something that is fading, the more animated the feelings become (KHW,47)

---

14.   I.e., organs of vision.

organs of clairvoyance are built out of the feelings and thoughts thus evoked

the soul world—the so-called 'astral' plane—begins to dawn upon him

growth and decay no longer remain facts, form themselves into spiritual lines and figures

the same spiritual figure will present itself to two souls

a blossoming flower, a growing animal, a dying tree will each conjure up a very definite form before his soul

anyone versed in occult science will describe the spiritual forms of the processes of growth and decay according to species, genus

the occult investigator must not lose himself in speculation as to the meaning of one thing or another (KHW,48)

he should not try to determine what the things mean, but should allow the things themselves to tell him (KHW,50)

so now his path[15] leads him *between* the phenomena of growing and withering[16]

---

B.

the pupil must also discriminate between sounds produced by anything called lifeless and sounds that come from a living creature (KHW,51)

he must concentrate his whole attention on what the sound from a living creature tells him of something that is foreign to his own soul: what is going on in the being from whom the sound proceeds

the pupil must learn to respond in this way to the whole of nature (KHW,52)

the pupil is now aware of a new language of the soul

---

15. In thought.
16. In their spiritual 'forms' on the 'astral' plane: i.e., the 'soul' plane.

the whole of nature begins to whisper her secrets

he begins to 'hear' with his soul

---

something more has to be added

of special importance is the way the pupil listens to others when they are speaking

while 'listening', his own inner self is absolutely silent

the pupil must silence all inner agreement or disagreement

doing so in particular cases deliberately chosen

pupils are enjoined to listen to the most contradictory views and to silence all positive agreement, all adverse criticism, suppressing every feeling of superiority (KHW,53)

the pupil learns gradually to merge himself into the being of another

he 'hears' through the words into the very soul of the other

perception of the inner word awakens (KHW,54)

it is to one who through selfless listening can become inwardly receptive in quietude and unmoved that the higher beings speak

all higher truths are attained through perception of the inner word

[17]to all that has here been said must be added the zealous study of what occult investigators communicate to the world

these teaching are drawn from living perception of the inner word

---

17.   To the other 'exercises' is now added 'study'.

they are living powers at work in your soul to make you clairvoyant (KHW,55)

———————————————

ENLIGHTENMENT is the result of simple processes

one who carries through the processes strictly can be led to a perception of the manifestations (i.e., the 'colours') of the inner light (the astral light)

one should direct one's whole attention to a comparison of the stone with the animal

no other thought, no other feeling must intrude to disturb the intensely attentive contemplation

the stone remains motionless; natural impulse—desire—causes the animal to change its place, is served by the animal's form (KHW,56)

the stone is fashioned by power that is void of desire (KHW,57)

one thinks deeply into such thoughts

two different kinds of feelings will arise in the soul

if the plant is included in the contemplation, the feeling emanating from it lies midway between the feeling that streams from the stone and the feeling that streams from the animal

out of these feelings and thoughts organs of clairvoyance are formed (KHW,57)

the spiritual world with its lines and figures (until now dark) through Enlightenment becomes light

'dark' and 'light' describe only approximately what is meant

every stone, plant, animal has its own definite nuance of colour

the 'colours' seen are of a spiritual kind

there are also the beings of the higher worlds—their 'colours' are often wonderful, also often horrible (KHW,58)

if a man has reached the point described here, the ways to a great deal are open to him (KHW,59)

———————————————

but, whoever has not learnt to wait in the highest and best sense of the word will never achieve results of real value (KHW,61)

the pupil must continually enhance his moral strength, his inner purity, his powers of observation

the pupil must take care that his compassion for the human and animal worlds, and his response to the beauty of nature, are increasing (KHW,59)

———————————————

let the pupil place before him a small seed of a plant (KHW,63)

let him reflect: intensify the right kind of thoughts while contemplating this object

"Out of this seed, if planted in the soil, there will grow a plant."

let him visualize the plant:

"what I am now picturing in my imagination will later be drawn out of the seed"

"is already secretly enfolded within it as the force of the whole plant"

in the artificial imitation of the seed no such force is present

it is to this invisible something that thought and feeling are now to be directed (KHW,64)

the invisible will become visible

already announces its presence in my thinking

in inner quiet the thought must be experienced, intensely felt

sufficient time must be allowed for the thought, and feeling united with it, to penetrate the soul

then after a time an inner force will make itself felt, will create a new power of perception

something formerly not seen is here revealed: the plant manifests in a spiritually visible way[18] (KHW,65)

---

from *Occult Science*

in spiritual training everything depends upon the concentration of the entire soul-life upon one visualization.

---

18.  One constant objective behind all such visualizations is suggested to us directly in another meditative 'exercise' which must be counted among the most important and the most effective Steiner gives us. We finds it in his *Occult Science* (pp.265-267):

"We visualize a plant as it roots in the earth...now we think of a human being beside this plant...we say that the human is indeed more perfect than the plant, but...the latter may appear to me in a certain sense more perfect than the human being...chaste...pure.... I now visualize how the green sap flows...an expression of the pure, passionless laws of growth. I then visualize how the red blood flows through the human veins, and how it is the expression of the instincts, desires, and passions...then I visualize further how the human being is capable of evolution: how he may purify and cleanse his instincts and passions through his higher soul powers. I visualize how, as a result of this, something base in these instincts and desires is destroyed and how the latter are reborn on a higher plane.... In my thoughts I look now...upon the rose and say, I see the red rose petal, I see the color of the green plant sap transformed into red...the symbol of a blood that is the expression of purified instincts and passions that have stripped off all that is base.... I now seek not merely to imbue my intellect with such thoughts but to bring them to life in my feelings.... It is of importance that we do not *without* feeling confront the thoughts that serve to construct such a symbolic visualization. After we have pondered on such thoughts and feelings for a time, we are to transform them into the following symbolic visualization. We visualize a black cross...a symbol of the destroyed base elements of instincts and passions, and at the center...seven red, radiant roses...the symbol of a blood that is the expression of purified, cleansed passions and instincts..."

This visualization must, by means of free will, be placed at the center of consciousness.

symbolic visualizations ... are formed through the soul's own energy.

what is essential is the fact that the visualization, through the way it is visualized,
liberates the soul from dependence on the physical. (OS,264)

In every case these means to inner meditation have the objective of liberating the
soul from sense-perception[19] (OS,269)

The symbols that are constructed in the above described manner do ... not yet
relate to anything real in the spiritual world.

They serve the purpose of detaching the human soul from sense-perception

I ... visualize something by means of forces in connection with which my senses
and my brain do not serve me as instruments.

[the pupil] may then say to himself: "My consciousness is not extinguished when
I disregard the sense-perceptions and ordinary intellectual thinking

I can lift myself out of them and then feel myself as a being *alongside* the one I
was previously". (OS,273)

The individual beholds first, therefore, what he has created. Thus, the first experience is, in a certain sense, self-perception.

The soul ... at first perceives itself in the world of pictures—imagina-
tions—which appear as a result of the exercises described.

Although these pictures appear as living in a new world, the soul must recognize
that they are, at the outset, nothing but the reflection of its own being, strengthened through the exercises

---

19.  By 'dissolving' the identity of subject and object (i.e., attachment of subject to
object). Cf. Coleridge on 'dissolution' above, pp.66-67.

[the soul] must also have developed such a power of will that it can extinguish, can eliminate these pictures from consciousness at any time.

The soul must be able to act within these pictures completely free and fully aware. (OS,274)

---

Only one group of inner imaginative experiences constitutes an exception to this possibility of extinction.

These experiences are *not* to be extinguished at this stage of spiritual training.

They correspond to the kernel of the soul's own being.

In regard to everything else the independence of the experiences mentioned must rule, and only after having acquired the ability to bring about this extinction does the student approach the true external spiritual world.

In place of what has been extinguished, something else appears that is recognized as spiritual reality.[20] (OS,275)

from *Knowledge of the Higher Worlds*

During all these exercises the individual must never lose his fully conscious self-control.

He must practise the same reliable thinking that he applies to the details of every-day life. (KHW,66)

---

20.   From this we may infer that progress or 'expansion' in spiritual vision (i.e., 'medita-tion') is the result of a continuous *series* of acts of 'dissolution' or 'extinction': exten-sive acts of 'will' in Coleridge's sense. (Cf. Novalis's reference to "the absolute independence and boundless propensity of meditation", cited by Prokofieff, *Eternal Individuality*, p.55)

'Dissolution' could and should be seen as a process of 'dying', with a kind of 'death' at every stage: a progressive 'dying' *to* the world, with continuous 'expansion' as the 'resurrection' that follows from this potentially.

In another part of the 'spiritual science' Steiner gives us, this process of 'dying' is referred to as the 'Consciousness-Soul' experience, in which we have been evolving since the early fifteenth century.

For an introductory account of this evolution, with specific reference to Shakes-peare's development as a tragic artist, see *Othello's Sacrifice* (pp.76ff).

The 'Imaginative-Soul' experience, or *Imagination* proper, represents merely a *first* distinct stage in the process of 'resurrection' or 'expansion' that potentially attends on the Consciousness-Soul experience.

Romanticism itself has only ever gotten this far as a literary-exoteric manifesta-tion, but Steiner's life-work will reveal that there are in fact two *further* stages, which he called *Inspiration* and *Intuition*—stages that, as far as I know, only Shakespeare anticipates prophetically in our literature (see *Sacrifice*).

In our time, this extensive activity of 'will' is directly expressed in the movement of Anthroposophy that Steiner was able to establish based on the findings from his own development. Here the *full* evolution or 'wisdom' available to 'man' (as Anthro-pos-Sophia) is made known, and *in* that 'wisdom' is the 'will' of man matured.

It was Steiner's repeated claim that a mere devotion to the concepts that Anthro-posophy brings forward, on the basis of this activity of will, was enough to kindle the power of Imagination in some degree at present and fully in due course. Hence, the great educative value of Anthroposophy for us today.

In the background of this entire historical development, as we learn from a more evolved form of Steiner's spiritual science, is the still *fuller* activity of 'will' in which mankind has shared, since the mystery of Golgotha, with Christ.

from *Occult Science*

the student who has reached the characterized stage by proper training is just as able to distinguish his own visualization from spiritual reality as a man with a healthy mind is able to distinguish the thought of a hot piece of iron from an actual one that he touches with his hand.

Healthy experience, and nothing else, shows the difference. (OS,280)

---

from *Knowledge*

let the pupil place before him a fully developed plant

let him fill his mind with the thought: The time will come when this plant will wither and die

but the plant will have developed seeds

in what I see something I do not see lies hidden

at present, I cannot see what preserves this plant from disappearance

this thought, imbued with the feeling that should go with it, will again develop in my soul a force which will become new vision

again there will grow out of the plant a kind of spiritual flame-form (KHW,67)

---

It would be a serious mistake for anyone to suppose he could reach his goal if the grain of seed or the plant were merely pictured, merely visualized in the imagination

the point is not that I arbitrarily create visions for myself, but that reality creates them in me

the truth must well up from the depths of my own soul

but, the magician who conjures forth the truth must be the actual beings whose spiritual reality I want to behold

now the pupil may proceed to the contemplation of man himself (KHW,69)

when the pupil passes from the stone, the plant and the animal up to man, union of the soul with the spiritual world takes place under all circumstances and leads on to Initiation (KHW,60)

(i)
Recall to mind someone whom you may have observed when he was filled with desire for some object

focus on the desire itself: when the desire was keenest, and it was still uncertain whether the object of the desire would be obtained

maintain the utmost inner calm in your own soul

be blind and deaf to everything else that is going on around you

take care that through the mental picture thus evoked a feeling is awakened in the soul (KHW,70)

you will succeed in bringing things to the point of experiencing in your own soul a feeling corresponding to the state of soul of the individual observed

this feeling elicits in your soul a force that becomes a spiritual perception of the other's state of soul

a picture will appear—the so-called astral embodiment of the state of soul caused by the desire

---

much depends upon treating such a spiritual perception with delicacy

know how to be silent about your spiritual experiences

be silent about them even to yourself

lend yourself freely to your spiritual perception—do not disturb yourself by pondering over it (KHW,71)

at the beginning your power of reflection is by no means on a level with your vision

only one who has already gained some certainty and steadiness in the observation of inner experiences can speak about them in such a way that his fellow-men will be stimulated

(ii)
Observe in the same way someone to whom the fulfilment of such a wish, the gratification of some desire, has been granted

the attainment of spiritual perception will also be possible here

such observation should be practised only by one who has already risen to the level at which he is fully convinced that thoughts are realities [i.e., 'orientation']

---

observing his fellow-men in this way, the pupil may succumb to a moral defect, may be become unloving, uncharitable

he must not allow himself to think of his fellow-men in a way that is incompatible with the highest reverence for human dignity and human liberty (KHW,72)

the thought that a human being could be merely an object of observation must never for a moment be entertained

every occult investigation of human nature goes hand in hand with a recognition that what lives in each human being is sacred and inviolable

---

the soul of anyone who has achieved the inner calm and tranquility necessary for such observation will undergo a great transformation the inner enrichment of his being gives confidence and composure to his outer behavior;

this will in turn react upon his soul, and he will be able to help himself further along the path

by following this path, the pupil comes nearer and nearer to the moment when he can take the first steps of Initiation (KHW,73)

---

the would-be initiate must bring with him a certain mature courage and fearlessness

he must go out of his way to find opportunities through which these qualities are developed

the pupil must be prepared to look danger calmly in the face

'to be frightened', 'to lack courage' are out of the question for him, at least in his inmost self

whoever presses forward to the higher mysteries sees things which the illusions of the senses conceal, things which, if he were unprepared, would throw him into utter disarray

the pupil must be able to endure this sight

he loses certain supports in the outer world which he owed to his entanglement in illusion (KHW,74)

---

in the world there are constructive and destructive forces

the veil screening the eyes of spirit must be removed

but man is himself interwoven with these forces

to the eyes of the seer, his own soul is revealed

the pupil must not lose strength: and only if he brings a surplus with him will his strength not fail

to this end, he must learn to maintain inner calm and steadiness in difficult circumstances

he must cultivate in himself a strong trust in the beneficent powers of existence

many motives which had actuated him hitherto will do so no longer (KHW,75)

he will have to develop quite new motives for thinking and acting

it is a question of cultivating this courage and this fearlessness in the inmost depths of the life of thought

the pupil must learn not to despair over failure

in this way, he struggles through to the conviction that the sources of strength in the universe on which he can draw are inexhaustible

he struggles ever onwards to the spirit which will lift him and support him (KHW,76)

---

If the exercises described in the preceding sections ... are practised rightly, certain changes take place in the so-called soul-organism (KHW,117)

The further the individual advances in his inner development the more clearly differentiated in structure will his soul-organism become. (KHW,118)

It extends from the interior of the head to the middle of the physical body.

It appears as a kind of independent body, possessing certain organs.

These organs are called by occultists 'wheels' (chakrams) or also 'lotus flowers'.

When a pupil begins his exercises, the lotus-flowers become brighter, and later on they begin to revolve. (KHW,119)

these flowers *are* the sense-organs of the soul and their revolution is an expression of the fact that supersensible perception has been achieved.

---

Now certain activities of the soul are connected with the development of these organs, and anyone who carries out these activities in a quite specific way contributes something to the development of the corresponding spiritual sense-organs[21] (KHW,120)

---

The development of the lotus-flowers alone does not ensure for him sufficient security in these higher worlds; he must have still higher organs at his disposal (KHW,139)

Mere mobility of the lotus-flowers does not suffice. The individual must be in a position to regulate and control independently and with full consciousness the movement of his spiritual organs.

he must acquire the faculty of hearing what is called the 'inner word', and this entails the development not only of the soul-body but also of the etheric body.

---

The latter is the fine, delicate body that is revealed to the clairvoyant as a kind of 'double' of the physical body. (KHW,140)

---

21.   Steiner presents a detailed and systematic account of these 'activities' of moral conduct in life, in *Knowledge of the Higher Worlds*, in the chapters: "Practical Aspects", "The Conditions of Esoteric Training", and especially, "Some Effects of Initiation" where their effects on a development of the organs of vision (the 'lotus-flowers') are systematically described. Such 'activities', or manner of life, are crucial to the pupil's training, indeed indispensable on the path to higher experience: "For while the special instructions, i.e., 'exercises', given in Spiritual Science activate the *maturing process*, the *form* is imparted by the manner of life, the 'activities', described above." (p.133)

the components of the etheric body are in continuous movement. Numberless currents pass through it in every direction, and by these currents life is sustained and regulated. (KHW,141)

---

If the pupil carries out the instructions given him, he brings into his etheric body currents and movements which are in harmony with the laws and evolution of the world to which man belongs.

Hence these instructions are always a reflection of the great laws of cosmic evolution. (KHW,143)

They consist of the above-mentioned and similar exercises in meditation and concentration.

---

A simple start is made designed, above all, to deepen and intensify intelligent, rational thinking.

This thinking is thereby made free and independent of all physical sense-impressions and experiences. It is concentrated, as it were, in a single point which is entirely under the person's control.

Thereby a provisional centre is created for the currents of the etheric body.

---

This centre is not yet in the region of the heart, but in the head

The only esoteric training that can be completely successful is one which first creates this centre.

If the centre were formed in the region of the heart from the very beginning, the incipient clairvoyant might certainly have glimpses of the higher worlds, but he would have no true insight into the connection of these higher worlds with our physical world.

And this is an unconditional necessity for man at the present stage of evolution.

The clairvoyant must not become a fancy-ridden visionary; he *must* keep solid ground under his feet.

---

The centre in the head, once duly established, is then transferred lower down, to the region of the larynx. (KHW,144)

Then the currents of the etheric body radiate from this region and illuminate the soul-space around the individual.

---

And now comes the time to give the whole system of currents and movements a centre in the region of the heart

---

at this point ... the stage is reached when the pupil can hear the 'inner word'. (KHW,145)

All things.... become as it were spiritually audible in their inmost nature and speak to him of their essential being.

He begins to participate in the life of his environment and can let it reverberate in the movements of the lotus flowers.

the spiritual world is entered.[22] (KHW,146)

---

A completely new life opens out for the individual when the development of his etheric body has begun in the way described

through his esoteric training he must receive at the right moment the enlightenment which enables him to find his bearings in his new existence. (KHW,150)

---

Within the world of forms ... (KHW,151)

[he] can now observe the inner content of his personality as outer world (KHW,152)

His own impulses and passions stand before him ... in forms ... of an animal or—less often—of a human character. (KHW,153)

from *Occult Science*

in the physical sense-world ... one ... finds the means of disposing of ... delusions when, with sound judgment, one takes into consideration all that may possibly contribute to an adequate factual explanation.

In the supersensible world this is not immediately possible (OS,334)

---

22.    This is a development in 'inspiration':
"The world of inspiration is...something quite new....Through *imagination* one learns to know the *soul*-expression of beings; through *inspiration* one penetrates into their inner *spiritual* nature. One recognizes above all a host of spiritual beings [through 'tones'] and discerns a great number of relationships between one being and another....
...observation in the world of inspiration may only be compared with *reading*; and the beings of the world of inspiration act upon the observer like the letters of an alphabet....
...Spiritual science, therefore, may call cognition through inspiration—speaking figuratively—the *reading of secret or occult script*" (*Occult Science*, pp.305-306).
Steiner also accounts for the *basis* of a development in inspiration; "I wish to feel within me all that my soul has done in order to bring an image into existence, but I do not wish to hold the image itself; I wish to live quite inwardly within my own activity, which has created the image. Thus, I do not intend to meditate on an image, but to dwell in my own image-creating soul activity....This then leads to cognition through inspiration." (*Occult Science*, p.312).
"The exercises for the attainment of *intuition* demand that the student cause not only the images, to which he has surrendered himself in acquiring imagination, to disappear from his consciousness, but also the life within his own soul activity into which he has immersed himself for the acquirement of inspiration. He should then literally retain *nothing* in his soul of previously known outer or inner experiences...
A time will come when the consciousness is *not* empty after the soul has discarded all inner and outer experiences, but when, after this discarding, something remains in consciousness as an effect, to which we then may surrender in meditation..." (*Occult Science*, p.320)

If one wants to observe a supersensible process, and approaches it with false judgment, one carries this judgment over into the process and it becomes so interwoven with the fact that it is impossible to distinguish the judgment from the fact

[the pupil] can exclude what comes from himself if he has first recognized the image of his own *Doppelganger*.

he acquires the ability to recognize, from the inner *quality* of a supersensible fact, whether it is reality or delusion.

Delusions of the supersensible world have qualities *in themselves* by which they are to be distinguished from realities, and it is important that the student of the spiritual know by which qualities he can recognize realities. (OS,335)

from *Knowledge of the Higher Worlds*

within this world of pictures he will soon learn something quite new.

His *lower self* is before him as a mirror-image only

but within this image there appears the true reality of the *higher Self.*[23]

The form of the spiritual Ego becomes visible out of the picture of the lower personality.[24]

---

23.   A first positive effect of the power of inspiration working through the world of imagination.
24.   We may refer the emergence of the higher Self to other words by Steiner (cited by Prokofieff, *Op.cit.*, p.209):
      "What is this human being who gives birth to the higher man within man, a man who represents a small world within the wider world, who is it that gives birth to the true, higher man out of a pure soul?…If we try to form a picture of the soul that gives birth to the higher man out of himself, out of the spiritual universe, we need only to call to mind the picture of the Sistine Madonna, the wonderful child in the arms of the Madonna. Thus in the Sistine Madonna we have before us a picture of the human soul as it is born out of the spiritual universe; and springing from this soul, the highest that a human being can bring forth—his spiritual birth, *the re-engendering of the creative activity of the world* that lies within him as potential."

Threads are then spun from the spiritual Ego to other, higher spiritual realities.

the individual finds it possible to establish a connection beween his higher Ego and lofty spiritual Beings. (KHW,155)

[the pupil] learns to know how his higher Self is connected with lofty spiritual Beings and forms a unity with them.[25] (KWH,158)

---

When the pupil has thus raised himself to a life in the higher 'I'—or rather *during* his acquisition of the higher consciousness—he will learn how to stir to life the force of spiritual perception in the organ lying in the region of the heart and control it

This perceptive force is an element of higher substantiality which proceeds from the organ in question and flows with radiant beauty through the moving lotus-flowers and the other channels of the developed etheric body.

Thence it radiates outwards into the surrounding spiritual world, rendering it spiritually visible (KHW,164)

---

Thus it will be seen that full consciousness of an object in the spiritual world is possible only when man himself casts upon it this spiritual light.

---

Now the 'I' which creates this organ of perception does not dwell within, but outside, the physical body

The heart-organ is only the place where the individual kindles from without this source of spiritual light.

---

25.  Through 'intuition': see *Occult Science*, p.344: "If the student of the spiritual has experienced intuition, he not only knows the images of the psycho-spiritual world, he cannot merely read their connections in the 'occult script', but he attains to knowledge of the spiritual beings themselves through whose co-operation the world, to which the human being belongs, comes into existence."

Were the light kindled elsewhere, the spiritual perceptions produced by it would have no connection with the physical world.

But all higher spiritual realities must be related to the physical world and man himself must act as a channel for them to flow into it.[26] (KHW,165)

---

During his dreams the individual is actually in a world different from that of his physical senses

he leads a second, unconscious life in that other world.

He engraves into it all his thoughts and perceptions.

These tracings become visible only when the lotus-flowers are developed. (KHW,162)

---

26.  "The heart-organ is only the place where the individual kindles from without this source of spiritual light.": see Sergei Prokofieff, *Eternal Individuality* (p.38): "This mystical secret of the etheric heart, which Rudolf Steiner was later to call 'heart-logic' (as opposed to 'head-logic') and by means of which he was able to accomplish all his spiritual research, was revealed to Novalis as though at one stroke of higher spiritual inspiration." (p.39) Cf. Novalis, Kluckhohn, III, 570, cited by Lindeman, *Op.cit.*: "the heart seems, as it were, to be the religious organ. Perhaps the higher creation of the productive heart is nothing other than heaven."

Prokofieff adds: "Rudolf Steiner goes on to say that, apart from this microcosmic stream of etherized human blood flowing from below upwards, from the heart to the head, there is a second, macrocosmic stream within man that flows from the spiritual world in the direction from above downwards, through the region of the head towards the heart...By day the 'intellectual' stream is dominant, from heart to head...while at night, during sleep, the second 'moral' stream is dominant, carrying all the moral impulses which he is to make manifest in his waking life into him from the macrocosm...[W]ith the help of right meditation [the entire process of spiritual development highlighted in this collection], man is able to lead the forces of the day stream over into the night stream, that is, the forces of waking consciousness living in the 'intellectual' stream into the 'moral' stream....He will then come to experience this conscious penetration into the world of night as a kind of real passage through death and resurrection in the 'moral fire'....It was through such a 'night' experience, an experience of 'dying and becoming', that Novalis passed..." (See *Hymns to the Night*.)

Developed lotus-flowers alone make it possible for manifestations not derived from the physical world to be imprinted in the same way.

And then the etheric body, when developed, brings full knowledge concerning these engraved impressions that are derived from other worlds.

This is the beginning of life and activity in a new world

[the pupil] is led to make the same observations during ordinary waking consciousness.

He will so train his receptivity for these spiritual impressions that they need no longer vanish in the face of the physical impressions, but will always be at hand for him and reach him in addition to the physical ones. (KHW,163)

when the experiences during sleep begin ... the moment of birth is approaching for the liberated soul which has literally become a new being (KHW,176)

_____

If the pupil continues the exercises connected with his training, he will find in due time that ... [i]solated conscious experiences begin to interrupt the complete insensibility of deep sleep. (KHW,172)

The things he reflects about during life, what he would like to understand in his environment but cannot grasp with the ordinary intellect—these are the things concerning which the experiences during sleep give enlightenment.

his mind tries to conceive and understand the connections between things (KHW,174)

he tries to grasp in ideas and concepts what his senses perceive.[27]

_____

27.  Note the integrity of Steiner's terms, consistent here with all that he had expounded before. This is the case with Steiner throughout his work. We note, here, especially *how* or *whence* 'ideas' originate.

More and more it seems to the pupil as though the solution of the riddles over which he ponders is whispered to him in the tones and words from a higher world.

And he is then able to connect with ordinary life whatever comes to him from a higher world.

What was formerly accessible only to his thought, now becomes actual experience, as living and real as any experience in the world of sense can be.

The spiritual world hitherto concealed from the pupil now resounds for him out of his environment. (KHW,175)

-----

Here again the pupil must bear in mind that these experiences during sleep must not be regarded as fully valid knowledge as long as he is not able to carry over his awakened higher soul into waking consciousness as well.[28] (KHW,176)

-----

the pupil must realize that he is dealing with separate, more or less unconnected spiritual experiences.

He should therefore beware of constructing out of them a complete whole or even a connected system of knowledge.

His right course is to strive for an ever clearer conception of the real experiences and to await the spontaneous emergence of new experiences which will link up of their own accord with those already present.

-----

28. Through the activity of the Imagination as a conscious act of will, as a later text makes clear:

"man's creative forces, the real human forces, can only be perceived by man when he becomes clairvoyant during sleep....These human creative forces have a very special relation to all the other forces of nature...We must imagine the world that surrounds us, which we know in the forces of nature throughout the mineral, plant and animal kingdoms, reduced down to nothing then down to below nothing. Then it is that those forces arise that are creatively active in man when he sleeps." (from *The Occult Significance of the "Bhagavad Gita"* (Spring Valley, N.Y.: Anthroposophic Press, pp.94-96). Cf., also, p.66 n.5 and p.87 n.13 above.

These experiences increasingly link themselves together of their own accord, without this true union being disturbed by all manner of combinations and conclusions which in any case would originate only in an intellect accustomed to the physical world. (KHW,177)

---

[29]Man must participate in the spirit in order to be able to carry its revelations into the world of the senses.

He transforms the Earth by implanting in it what he has discovered in the spiritual world.

because man can work upon the Earth in a true sense only if he is a participator in those worlds where the creative forces lie concealed—for these reasons he should have the will to ascend to the higher worlds. (KHW,182)

---

And just as the child, out of a dim instinct, acquires forces requisite for life, so can man acquire the powers of the spiritual world before the higher Self is born.

without inner application to the findings of Spiritual Science, there is no chance whatever of acquiring genuine higher knowledge.

Insight into these teachings, based on a feeling for truth and clear, sound, comprehensive judgment, is possible even before spiritual things are actually seen.

One must study the testimonies of mystical knowledge to begin with, and through this study prepare oneself for vision.

A person who has vision without such preparation would be like a child born with eyes and ears but without a brain.

The world of sounds and colours would be spread out before him, but he would be unable to make anything of it. (KHW,157)

---

29.   Here, as elsewhere, Steiner explains why higher knowledge is necessary.

The efforts required for concentration and meditation must therefore be accurately and carefully maintained, for they are indeed the laws governing the germination and fruition of the higher being of soul. (KHW,176)

---

Certain things and facts belonging to the higher worlds will inevitably come into contact with the would-be Initiate.

But he will be able to see and hear them only if he has come to perceive spiritual forms of colours, tones and so on, described in the sections on Preparation and Enlightenment.

the would-be Initiate learns how the things of nature and living beings manifest themselves to the spiritual ear and the spiritual eye.

In a certain way these beings and things then lie disclosed—naked—before the beholder. (KHW,78)

They are hidden from sensory perception as though behind a veil.

The falling away of this veil for the would-be Initiate is connected with a process known as 'spiritual burning away' [or] the 'trial by Fire' (KHW,79)

---

The pupil meets the Lesser Guardian[30]

A truly terrible, spectral Being confronts the pupil, and he will need all that presence of mind and faith in the reliability of his path of knowledge which he has had ample opportunity to acquire in the course of his training. (KHW,191)

However terrible the form assumed by the Guardian, it is only the effect of the pupil's past life, only his own character awakened into independent existence outside himself. (KHW,196)

from *Occult Science*

---

30.  The first form in which the higher 'self' presents itself to him, i.e., through the lower 'self' or *Doppelganger* (see above, p.113).

If, without encountering the 'guardian of the threshold', man were to enter the world of soul and spirit, he might fall prey to deception after deception. For he would never be able to distinguish between what he himself has carried over into that world and what in reality belongs to it. (OS,332)

from *Knowledge of the Higher Worlds*

The aim of the pupil's preparation must be to enable him to endure the terrible sight without a trace of timidity, and at the moment of the meeting to feel his strength so increased that he can consciously undertake to make himself responsible for the ennoblement of the Guardian. (KHW,197)[31]

from *Occult Science*

He has to direct and lead with his new-born self what he is in his ordinary self and which appears to him in an image.

A sort of battle against the *Doppelganger* will result.... [t]o establish the right relationship to this *Doppelganger* and not permit him to do anything that is not under the influence of the new-born ego ... (OS,338)

from *Knowledge*

---

31. "As a rule we cannot enter the spiritual worlds without passing through a deep upheaval in our souls....Emotions that are generally spread out over many moments, over long periods of living, whose permanent effect on the soul is therefore weaker—such feelings are concentrated in a single moment and storm through us with tremendous force when we enter the occult worlds...[W]e experience a kind of inner shattering...fear...anxiety...horror....Such a person must be prepared so that he may experience this upheaval as a necessary event in his soul life without its encroaching on his bodily life and health, because his body must not suffer a like upheaval....The soul forces we need for everyday living, our ordinary intellectual powers, even those of imagination, of feeling and will—these too must not be allowed to become unbalanced. The upheaval...must take place in far deeper layers of the soul, so that we go through our external life as before, without anything being noticed in us outwardly...That is what it means to be ripe for occult development..." (from *Occult Significance of the "Bhagavad Gita"*, pp.17-18)

   Cf. Shakespeare's own experience as I present this in *Othello's Sacrifice*, see pp.110ff.

the higher training ... makes it possible for the pupil to advance to the Threshold, and at the same time equips him to find the necessary strength at the right moment.

Indeed, the training can have such a harmonious effect that the entry into the new life is freed from any agitating or tumultuous effects.[32] (KHW,201)

---

If, after completing the Trial by Fire, the candidate wishes to continue the esoteric training, a certain script, generally adopted in such training, must be disclosed to him.

The occult script reveals itself to the soul when the soul has developed spiritual perception, for it is inscribed enduringly in the spiritual world. (KHW,80)

The signs of the occult script are not arbitrarily devised, but correspond to the forces actively working in the world

The language of things is learned through these signs.[33]

The signs ... correspond to the figures, colours, tones ... learnt ... during the stages of Preparation and Enlightenment.

Now for the first time [the pupil] is beginning to read in the higher world.

The separate shapes, tones, and colours are now revealed to him as forming a great interconnected whole.

Now for the first time he has real certainty in observing the higher worlds.

---

32.  As may be observed in the case of Novalis, Kluckhohn, I,135: "Away fled the splendor of earth and my sorrow along with it. My pain flowed together into a new and unfathomable world. You, spirit joy of Night, slumber of heaven, came over me. The place lifted itself softly upward; over the place hovered my free new-born spirit..."
33.  The point to which German romantic philosophy (and all other philosophies) needed to come before it could have any basis for pronouncing on 'things' and their relation to human consciousness.

now, at last, a systematic understanding is possible between the candidate and the Initiate in the domain of higher knowledge.

---

Through this language the pupil becomes acquainted also with certain rules of conduct, and with certain duties of which he had known nothing. (KHW,81)

he can perform actions endowed with a significance such as the actions of one who is not initiated can never possess.

He acts from out of the higher worlds. (KHW,82)

Should [the pupil] in the course of his action, introduce any element of his own wishes, opinions, and so forth, or should he for one moment evade the laws he has recognized to be right in order to indulge his own arbitrary will, the result would be altogether different from what should properly come about.

confusion would set in. (KHW,84)

Throughout this Trial [the 'Trial by Water'] ... the candidate has abundant opportunity to develop his self-control.

to produce a particular effect in these worlds we must have ourselves completely under control ... must follow the right principles only and be subject to no arbitrary impulse.[34] (KHW,85)

---

[in] the third Trial [the 'Trial by Air'].... [e]verything is left in his own hands.

nothing prompts him to act.

he must find his way quite alone, from out of himself.[35]

---

34. The consequence of 'extinction'.
35. In 'intuition'.

All that is necessary is that the candidate shall be able quickly to come to terms with his own nature, for here he must find his 'higher self' in the truest sense of the word.

He must instantly decide to listen in all things to the inspiration of the spirit.

Whatever keeps him from listening to the voice of the spirit must be boldly overcome. (KHW,87)

---

[later] the candidate learns how to apply the occult teaching, how to place it in the service of humanity.

He begins really to understand the world.

It is ... a question of ... presenting [the higher truths] in the right way and with the appropriate tact.

in the service of the world as far and as adequately as is possible[36] (KHW,89)

---

from *Theosophy*

Goethe ... says: "It is really in vain that we try to express the nature of a thing. We become aware of effects and a complete history of these effects would indeed embrace the nature of that thing.

Colors and light are ... linked in the most precise relationship, but we must think of them both as belonging to the whole of nature ... engaged in revealing itself

Nature thus speaks downwards ... to known, unknown and unrecognized senses.... is nowhere dead or silent." (TH,72)

---

36.  A task to which Steiner would devote his life. In this way, Rudolf Steiner *fulfils* the project with which Coleridge had once identified himself, though he could not accomplish it: as on p.69: "and I will cause the world of intelligences and the whole system of their representations to rise before you...".

This thought of Goethe corresponds entirely with the views of spiritual science as set forth here. (TH,73)

Goethe does not mean that we perceive only the effects of a thing.... He means rather that one should not speak at all of a 'hidden being'. The being is not behind its manifestation. On the contrary, it comes into view through the manifestation. (TH,72)

This being, however, is in many respects so rich that it can manifest itself to other senses in still other forms.

What reveals itself does belong to the being, but because of the limitations of the senses, it is not the whole being.

so does a man develop in himself soul and spiritual organs of perception through which the soul and spiritual worlds are opened to him.

For the development of his higher senses, however, he must work himself. If he wishes to perceive the soul and spirit worlds, he must develop soul and spirit, just as nature has developed his body

Such a development of the higher organs ... is not unnatural because in the higher sense all that man accomplishes belongs also to nature (TH,73)

---

to the man who awakens the higher sense in himself.... [t]he world appears ... with new qualities, events, and facts, about which the physical senses reveal nothing.

through these higher organs he adds nothing arbitrarily to reality, but ... without them the essential part of this reality would have remained hidden from him.[37]

---

37.   And in reaching this "essential part" (through the 'idea'), we never leave the realm of the 'given'. We thus enter the soul and spirit worlds, with Steiner, staying always *within* the 'given'.

the previously dark world flashes out in lights and colors ... [T]hings that previously were only corporeal phenomena reveal their soul and spirit qualities to anyone who is awakened in soul and spirit.

this world then becomes filled with other occurrences and beings that remain completely unknown to those whose soul and spirit senses are unawakened. (TH,74)

Just as a photograph grows intelligible and living to us when we have become so intimately acquainted with the person photographed that we know his soul,

so can we really understand the corporeal world only when we gain a knowledge of its soul and spirit basis.

For this reason it is advisable to speak ... first about the higher worlds ... and only then judge the physical from the viewpoint of spiritual science. (TH,76)

# Suggested Further Reading

(Lecture Cycles by Steiner)

*Theosophy of the Rosicrucian*

*The Apocalypse of St. John*

*Macrocosm and Microcosm*

*The Gospel of St. Matthew*

(By other authors)

A.C. Harwood, *The Faithful Thinker*

Sergei O. Prokofieff, *The Heavenly Sophia and the Being Anthroposophia*

The editions of the texts I have used in this collection were those from which I had been working in the period when the collection was put together over ten years ago. They are the editions most likely to be found in university libraries today. Most of these editions have since been superceded, but in the case of some the pagination may be the very same. A full and up-to-date list of works by Rudolf Steiner and other anthroposophical writers may be obtained from the following:

Rudolf Steiner Press, Forest Row, England

Steiner Books, Great Barrington, Massachusetts, USA

Tri-Fold Books, Guelph, Ontario, Canada

# A Further Commentary on Rudolf Steiner's Spiritual Science

## I

Steiner's *Knowledge of the Higher Worlds* focuses principally on 'exercises' and 'activities' that account respectively for the 'maturing process' and the proper 'formation' of our developing 'soul-organs' of vision, traditionally designated in the East as 'lotus flowers'.

The exercises themselves constitute the focus of an activity in 'concentration' and 'meditation' whose aim is "to deepen and intensify intelligent, rational thinking" (TS, 103) so as, first and foremost, to establish a distinct *centre* of etheric life in the so-called 'etheric brain' (TS, 103).

The exercises are continually accompanied by 'study' of "what occult investigators have communicated to the world" (TS, 90)—"the testimonies of mystical knowledge" (TS, 111)—which for our time consist first of the findings of Steiner's own Spiritual Science.

Thus an inner application to the concepts and ideas of Spiritual Science as Steiner himself gives this to us is in itself a formative force in establishing that strong centre of thinking power called the etheric brain.

In this formation, then, we have a first development of the thinking spirit.

The actual development of *vision*, however, depends on a proper formation of the so-called lotus flowers or soul-organs of vision.

Here the activities of moral conduct in life are indispensable.

121

The so-called 'eightfold path' lies behind the development of the sixteen-petalled lotus in the region of the larynx.

Application to the 'six virtues" (also known as 'the six attributes', 'the six qualities') lies behind the development of the twelve-petalled lotus in the region of the heart.

## II

As for the eightfold path, Steiner himself expands (KHW,121ff) on: right views, right judgment, right speech. Behind all three lies the power of thinking itself.

Thus, *right views* depend on our seeing in *every* idea "a definite message instructing [one] concerning things of the outer world, and [one] should not be satisfied with ideas devoid of such significance" (KHW,121)

As for *right judgment*: "[The pupil] should have well-considered *grounds* for everything he does" (122)

*right speech*: "He never speaks without *grounds* for what he says." (122)

Steiner also elaborates on the other five 'functions' on this path:

*right action*: "his actions ... harmonize with those of his fellow-men" (122)

*right habits*: "He looks upon life as a means for work ... He regulates his habits, the care of his health and so on ..." (123)

*right vocation*: "he sets before himself aims connected with the ideals and the great duties of a human being" (123). [cf. Steiner on 'detachment']

*right mindfulness*: "endeavour[s] to learn from life as much as possible" (123). [cf. Steiner on 'devotion', TS, 82]

*right contemplation*: "take[s] prudent counsel with himself ... form[s] and test[s] the basic principles of his life ..." (124)

Steiner then expounds on 'the six virtues' (KHW,129ff):

(i) inner control of the course taken by thoughts (ii) control of actions (iii) endurance (iv) tolerance (v) impartiality (vi) equanimity.

### III

While the sixteen-petalled lotus and the twelve-petalled lotus are in process of formation, our power of thinking, with its centre in the etheric brain, is also in process of extending *its* influence in a way that corresponds with the development of these flowers.

First, an etheric organ is formed likewise in the region of the larynx, followed by the formation of the 'etheric heart'.

A proper maturation of the soul-organs (i.e., 'flowers') in fact presupposes proper establishing first of these etheric organs.

With the formation of the etheric heart, the 'inner word' is first heard. (KWH,146)

At this point, Steiner proposes a reading (study) of the sermons of the Buddha and of the Gospels.

Formation of the etheric heart has its basis in 'love of inner freedom'—'the longing for liberation' (KWH,147,149)

This so-called 'habit' itself represents a development of 'concentration and meditation', or 'expansion', in the Romantic sense.

*         *         *

Steiner distinguishes in fact four 'habits':

1. discrimination between truth and semblance

2. right valuing of what is true

3. the 'six virtues' as a whole

4. 'love of inner freedom'

The first two habits summarize the *basis* of the eightfold path; the third (i.e., the six virtues) one might say *compounds* that path; while the power of thinking *runs through* the whole like a golden thread, being at the origin of the entire development both in moral conduct and in expanded vision.

## IV

Developing to this point, we take possession of ourselves first as 'soul-and-spirit' beings.

From here, the influence spreads further to possession of our experience in the sense world.

Control of sense impressions (through control of the five senses) corresponds to the development of the ten-petalled lotus flower in the region of the stomach. (KHW,134)

Having in this way extended the influence of thinking as spiritual activity through both the soul *and* the body, the pupil reaches an end-point of 'equilibrium' corresponding to the development of the six-petalled lotus in the region of the abdomen.

With this, stability of vision is achieved.

## V

With development of the sixteen-petalled lotus, spiritual 'lines and figures' come to discernment (recognizable to one's *thinking* power) in the astral or soul world. To these lines and figures, development of the twelve-petalled lotus in the region of the heart adds a perception of 'warmth' (or, *feeling* quality); while the ten-petalled lotus in the region of the stomach adds the perception of 'light and colour' (or, *will* quality).

With this, one has begun to penetrate the 'astral' or soul world in 'imaginative' vision.

With the perception afforded by the six-petalled lotus, all astral manifestations of spiritual being now emerge in their own 'independent life and existence'

(KHW,139), bringing with this the threat of disequilibrium in the soul of the pupil.

That threat, however, is now countered precisely by that force of 'equilibrium' to which the pupil has in the meantime won through, the result of his taking thorough possession of his powers of soul and body.

Possession of these powers takes the form of an etheric 'illumination' of these same powers proceeding from the 'purifying' force of thinking itself.

Something of this 'illuminating' function is suggested to us in the structural 'congruency' that obtains between the astral organs and the etheric organs simultaneously in process of being activated: after a strong centre is first established in the etheric brain, the sixteen-petalled lotus as astral organ becomes active, to be immediately 'illuminated' by the etheric organ likewise situated in the region of the larynx, and so on ...

## VI

Congruency is itself but a feature of the 'lawfulness' underlying the whole development in vision, grounded as this development is originally in the ideal lawfulness of thinking itself.

Thus the 'equanimity' that has served to establish the twelve-petalled lotus, itself immediately illuminated by the etheric organ in that region (the etheric heart), as a crowning soul 'virtue' already paves the way for the 'equilibrium' of spirit, soul and body that is fully discovered in the region of the abdomen when the six-petalled lotus comes into activity.

The climax to this effect of 'congruency' takes place where the astral and etheric developments meet, in the region of the heart; from here, the etheric heart extends its illuminating influence into every region of soul vision—through each and every one of the lotus flowers. In doing so, it makes central use itself of the twelve-petalled lotus: hence, the importance Steiner attaches to a proper development especially of this soul-organ, and so to the 'six virtues' that help to establish it in this region. (KWH,143)

VII

It is also from this region of the heart that the true form of the higher spiritual Ego finally appears from within the image of the lower (astral) self.

This is to see the development from the point of view of man and <u>microcosm</u>; <u>macro</u>cosmically, the development is also reflected to the pupil in the simultaneous emergence (KWH, 208) of the higher Guardian as independent Being from within the image of the lower Guardian (or Doppelganger).

Through the guidance of the Higher Guardian, a further connection is now established between the pupil's higher Ego and the Egos of other divine-spiritual Beings (KWH,155) through the present activation of the two-petalled lotus in the region of the forehead. This is the last such soul organ to be activated, the etheric illumination spreading out still further from this region after proceeding to it from the region of the heart (KHW,143).

Two 'worlds" are now distinguishable.

On the one hand, perceptible to the *incipient* higher ego (the ego in the process of appearing) are the astral 'forms' of crystals, plants, animals and man (in his desiring aspect); the 'forms' also of one's own lower self, as well as of certain lower and higher beings who never enter physical existence (KWH,58-59)—i.e., elemental beings, and other beings intermediate between men and angels. All 'forms' are distinguished and identified by their respective soul 'colours', i.e., by the distinctive soul impressions they give with which one first acquaints oneself through Preparation and Enlightenment, which *compare* to the impressions colours make on us.

On the other hand, the spiritual 'forces' behind the astral 'forms' become perceptible with the actual *birth* of the higher ego and its *further* expansion along *with* the higher Beings through whom these 'forces' are given or revealed. In this higher 'spirit' world, the form of perception is *purely* spiritual; that is, it emerges from the etheric illuminated by now from within its own world.

## VIII

Thus do soul-world and spirit-world come to manifestation as the actual production of thinking in the soul.

They come progressively to manifestation as the result of a continuous series of acts of 'will' innate to thinking in its pure, or ideal, function.

In *Theosophy*, Steiner speaks of the 'consciousness-soul', as the highest 'soul' member in which the thinking ego expresses itself. The 'consciousness-soul', he says, 'is in touch with the self-existent truth that is independent of all antipathy and sympathy'.

On the other hand, the 'spirit self', as the first of the 'spirit'-members, 'bears within it the same truth, but taken up into and enclosed by the 'I', individualized by it, and absorbed into the independent being of the individual'. (TH,30)

Thus, long before the higher Ego is actually born, the thinking ego or I already stands, in the 'consciousness-soul', in direct relation to the spirit as self-existent truth. It also stands in direct relation to the spirit in the 'spirit self' in its own individualized truth.

## IX

The process of *growing into* the truth is, then, as follows.

From beyond the world of 'forms' that belong to the soul-world, the ego receives ideas (intuitions) as an extension into waking-day consciousness of the 'inspirations' first gathered from the realm of deep dreamless sleep. [see TS, 109]

Though these 'inspirations' contain first the ideas which one comes into possession of in waking-day consciousness, they also carry within themselves that whole potential for 'illumination' which at a certain point comes to expression in those revelations of the spirit-world that follow from the expansion with divine-spiritual Beings.

Astral 'tracings' are gathered from the realm of dream life; they first come to expression in the lines and figures that at a certain point are discerned out of the astral, to unfold later into full perception of the soul-world.

We recall that by then the higher Ego is born; indeed, there can be no revelations of the spirit-world without this birth.

While the soul-world and spirit-world are thus in process of revealing themselves, knowledge is gathered about the various soul members: sentient soul, intellectual soul and consciousness soul, seen and recognized as three distinct soul members, though each grows out of the other.

Similarly, three spirit-members are identified as the spirit-self, life-spirit and spirit-man.

This experience has its corollary in knowledge of the seven regions of the soul and the seven regions of spiritland, until we reach the real home of the higher Ego in the fifth region of spiritland, from which the full 'vista' of evolution begins to emerge as given in *Theosophy of the Rosicrucian*.

*How* the vista is given is described further in Steiner's *Apocalypse*.

Perception of this vista begins then in 'lower Devachan' (in the fifth region of spiritland), but it is not fully established until one rises into 'upper Devachan' (the sixth and seventh regions of spiritland), as *Theosophy of the Rosicrucian* makes clear.

From here it would be a matter of following Steiner's own development in vision further, as his lectures and works convey this to us in such tremendous detail from stage to stage (an outline of what to read from *Theosophy* onwards has been given above).

978-0-595-45714-4
0-595-45714-2